GRAMMAR BOOK

Intermediate level (CEFR A2/B1)

Table of Contents

1.	Asking questions	1
2.	Adjectives and prepositions	11
3.	Conditional clauses	16
4.	Future tenses	30
5.	Passive voice	34
6.	Reported speech	46
7.	Present perfect progressive	59
8.	Past perfect simple	66
9.	Mixed Tenses	79
10.	Word Order	90
11.	Gerund or infinitive	98

ASKING QUESTIONS

Who - asking for people and animals: subject: no do, does, did

Jane opened the door.   Who opened the door?

Tom helped in the garden.   Who helped in the garden?

Who - asking for people and animals: object: do, does, did

They greet their teacher.   Who do they greet?

He asked Mary about the burglary.   Who did they ask about the burglary?

What - asking for a thing: subject: no do, does, did

His ankle hurt.   What hurts?

The flower pot fell on the floor.   What fell on the floor?

What - asking for things: object: do, does, did

She usually wears jeans.   What does she usually wear?

They built a castle in the sand.   What did they build in the sand?

Whose - asking for the 2nd case

This is Peter's pencil.   Whose pencil is this?

Carol's father was a drummer.   Whose father was a drummer?

When - asking for the time

I saw her yesterday.   When did you see her?

They came home at midnight.   When did they come home?

Where - asking for the place

He flew to Manchester.   Where did he fly?

He lives in a big house.   Where does he live?

Why - asking for a reason

He stayed at home because he was ill.   Why did he stay at home?

They like him because he is always friendly.   Why do they like him?

How - asking for the manner

He drove fast.   How did he drive?

My holidays were great.   How were your holidays?

How long - asking for a period of time
They stayed there <u>for a week</u>.　　　　　　　　How long did they stay there?
He lived in London <u>for a year</u>.　　　　　　　　How long did he live in London?

How many - asking for an exact amount
In this factory work <u>500</u> people.　　　　　　　How many people work in this factory?
<u>50</u> kids were at his party.　　　　　　　　　　How many kids were at his party?

How much - asking for not exact amount
He gets <u>10 pounds</u> pocket money a month.　　　How much pocket money does he get a month?
She bought <u>three bottles</u> of wine.　　　　　　How much wine did she buy?

How often - asking for frequency
They play tennis <u>twice a week</u>.　　　　　　　How often do they play tennis?
She meets him <u>every Friday</u>.　　　　　　　　How often does she meet him?

ASKING QUESTIONS 1

Ask for the underlined words. Form questions in the present simple.

1. The children go to the mall every week.
   _____

2. They sell 20 kilos of sugar a day.
   _____

3. He does his workout every morning.
   _____

4. The boys play football.
   _____

5. He lives in a big house.
   _____

6. The two women come from Brazil.
   _____

7. They usually work carefully.
   _____

8. The jacket is 50 dollars.
   _____

9. He likes his dog.
   _____

10. She goes to the bakery every Sunday morning.
    _____

11. They always get to the airport by taxi.
    _____

12. They go shopping once a week.
    _____

ASKING QUESTIONS 2

Ask for the underlined words. Form questions in the past simple.

1. Jane opened the door.
   _____

2. The dog ran over to the children.
   _____

3. The cat ate the fish.
   _____

4. The flower pot fell on the floor.
   _____

5. They met at the station.
   _____

6. She found Pamela's key.
   _____

7. Two policemen entered the room.
   _____

8. They came late because they had caused an accident.
   _____

9. The men came a little closer.
   _____

10. His car broke down.
    _____

11. They took the children home.
    _____

12. She ate two packets of crisps.
    _____

ASKING QUESTIONS 3

Ask for the underlined words.

1. He gives <u>Harry</u> a nice present.
   _____

2. They have got <u>five</u> cats.
   _____

3. They wrote down <u>the address</u>.
   _____

4. They water <u>our flowers and vegetables</u>.
   _____

5. Andy did his homework <u>very quickly</u>.
   _____

6. <u>My mum</u> pays for the ticket.
   _____

7. He kicked the ball <u>high into the air</u>.
   _____

8. They had <u>cameras</u>.
   _____

9. <u>Frank</u> bought an expensive car.
   _____

10. She ate <u>an apple</u>.
    _____

11. This flower smells <u>good</u>.
    _____

12. He repaired everything <u>carefully</u>.
    _____

ASKING QUESTIONS 4

Ask for the underlined words.

1. Tom lived in Chicago.
___

2. He drank some lemonade.
___

3. They stayed at a hotel.
___

4. Sandra went to the hill.
___

5. They cut the grass.
___

6. The kids heard a terrifying noise.
___

7. The guests made an awful mess.
___

8. The twins watched the movie yesterday.
___

9. They went home because they were tired.
___

10. We call Mary very weekend.
___

11. He stays at a hotel.
___

12. She took the umbrella because it was raining.
___

ASKING QUESTIONS 5

Ask for the underlined words.

1. The students put the books into their bags.
   _____

2. She wore black jeans last Tuesday.
   _____

3. Tina lives in a small village in Wales.
   _____

4. They went up 1860 steps to the top.
   _____

5. We took the elevator.
   _____

6. I get my pocket money from my dad.
   _____

7. This computer game has four levels.
   _____

8. I stayed up until twelve.
   _____

9. She copied the story.
   _____

10. He warmed his hands.
    _____

11. Tim and Susan fell in love.
    _____

12. We wrote lots of stories for her.
    _____

ASKING QUESTIONS 6

Ask for the underlined words.

1. <u>He</u> made a big mistake.
   _____

2. They danced <u>till the morning</u>.
   _____

3. It began <u>three years ago</u>.
   _____

4. He dropped the cup <u>on the floor</u>.
   _____

5. The lesson passed <u>quickly</u>.
   _____

6. He ran <u>across the street</u>.
   _____

7. She said it <u>very politely</u>.
   _____

8. I spent my holidays <u>in Switzerland</u>.
   _____

9. I play <u>three times a week</u>.
   _____

10. <u>My brother</u> teaches me a lot.
    _____

11. They gave up <u>on Monday</u>.
    _____

12. They started <u>the climb</u> on Sunday morning.
    _____

ASKING QUESTIONS 1

1. Who goes to the mall every week?
2. How many kilos of sugar a day do they sell?
3. What does he do every morning?
4. Who plays football?
5. Where does he live?
6. Who comes from Brazil?
7. How do they usually work?
8. How much is the jacket?
9. Who does he like?
10. Where does she go every Sunday morning?
11. How do they always get to the airport?
12. How often do they go shopping?

ASKING QUESTIONS 2

1. Who opened the door?
2. Where did the dog run?
3. What did the cat eat?
4. What fell on the floor?
5. Where did they meet?
6. Whose key did she find?
7. What did two policemen enter?
8. Why did they come late?
9. Who came a little closer?
10. What broke down?
11. Who did they take home?
12. How many packets of crisps did she eat?

ASKING QUESTIONS 3

1. Who does he give a nice present?
2. How many cats have they got?
3. What did they write down?
4. What do they water?
5. How did Andy do his homework?
6. Who pays for the ticket?
7. Where did he kick the ball?
8. What did they have?
9. Who bought an expensive car?
10. What did she eat?
11. How does this flower smell?
12. How did he repair everything?

ASKING QUESTIONS 4

1. Where did Tom live?
2. What did he drink?
3. Where did they stay?
4. Where did he go?
5. What did they cut?
6. What did the kids hear?
7. What did they make?
8. When did the twins watch the movie?
9. Why did they go home?
10. Who do you call very weekend?
11. Where does he stay?
12. Why did she take the umbrella?

ASKING QUESTIONS 5

1. Where did the students put their books?
2. When did she wear black jeans?
3. Where does Tina live in Wales?
4. How many steps did they go up to the top?
5. What did you take?
6. What do you get from your dad?
7. What does this computer game have?
8. How long did you stay up?
9. What did she copy?
10. What did he warm?
11. Who fell in love?
12. What did you write for her?

ASKING QUESTIONS 6

1. Who made a big mistake?
2. How long did they dance?
3. When did it begin?
4. Where did he drop the cup?
5. How did the lesson pass?
6. Where did he run?
7. How did she say it?
8. Where did you spend your holidays?
9. How often do you play?
10. Who teaches you a lot?
11. When did they give up?
12. What did they start on Sunday morning?

ADJECTIVES WITH PREPOSITIONS

nice / kind / good / stupid / silly / intelligent / clever / sensible / (im)polite / rude / unreasonable OF someone (to do something)
Examples: Thank you it was very **nice / kind of** you to help me.
It's **stupid of** her to go out without a coat.

nice / kind / good / (im)polite / rude / (un)pleasant / (un)friendly / cruel TO someone
Examples: She has always been very **nice / kind to** me.
Why are you so **rude / unfriendly to** Ann?

angry / furious ABOUT something // **WITH** someone **FOR** something
Examples: Why are you so **angry about** it?
They were **furious with** me **for** not inviting them to my party.

pleased / disappointed / satisfied WITH something
Examples: I was **pleased with** the present you gave me.
Were you **disappointed with** your examination results?

bored / fed up WITH something
Example: You get **bored / fed up with** doing the same thing every day.

surprised / shocked / amazed / astonished AT / BY something
Example: Everyone was **surprised by / at** the news.

excited / worried / upset ABOUT something
Example: Are you **excited about** going on holiday next week?

afraid / scared / frightened / terrified OF someone / something
Example: Are you **afraid of** dogs?

proud / ashamed OF someone / something
Example: I'm not **ashamed of** what I did.

good / bad / excellent / brilliant / hopeless AT (doing) something
Example: I'm not very **good at** repairing things.

married TO someone
Example: Linda is **married to** an American.

sorry ABOUT something
Example: I'm **sorry about** the noise last night.

sorry FOR doing something
Example: I'm **sorry for** shouting at you yesterday.

be / feel sorry FOR someone
Example: I feel **sorry for** George.

famous FOR something
Example: Florence is **famous for** its art treasures.

responsible FOR something
Example: Who was **responsible for** this noise last night?

interested IN something
Example: Are you **interested in** art?

fond OF something / someone
Example: Mary is **fond of** animals.

full OF something
Example: The letter was **full of** mistakes.

short OF something
Example: I'm a bit **short of** money.

keen ON something
Example: We stayed at home because Mary wasn't very **keen on** going out in the rain.

similar TO something
Example: Your writing is **similar to** mine.

crowded WITH (people...)
Example: The trains in the morning are usually very **crowded with** students.

ADJECTIVES WITH PREPOSITIONS 1

Complete with the correct prepositions. Fill in **for**, **of**, **to**, **about** or **at**.

1. She is brilliant _____ repairing things.
2. She is nice, but I don´t want to get married _____ her.
3. It's very nice _____ you to lend me your car.
4. He is married _____ his best friend's sister.
5. Why are you always so rude _____ your parents?
6. It wasn´t very polite _____ him to leave without saying thank you.
7. I can´t understand people who are cruel _____ animals.
8. I have to stop to talk to you. I'm a bit short _____ time.
9. She is excellent _____ skiing.
10. Your shoes are similar _____ mine, but they are not exactly the same.
11. We´ve got enough to eat. The fridge is full _____ food.
12. I felt sorry _____ the children because it rained every day.
13. He said he was sorry _____ the situation, but there was nothing he could do.
14. She is bad _____ surfing.
15. Our house is similar _____ theirs.
16. I feel sorry _____ him because it wasn't his fault.
17. It would be clever _____ you to study more.
18. France is also very famous _____ its wine.
19. The streets were crowded _____ people.
20. She was very upset _____ not being invited to the party.

ADJECTIVES WITH PREPOSITIONS 2

Complete with the correct prepositions. Fill in **by**, **for**, **of**, **with**, **on** or **in**.

1. She is very terrified _____ spiders.

2. We enjoyed our holidays, but we were disappointed _____ our hotel.

3. I was surprised _____ the way he behaved.

4. He is very fond _____ animals.

5. She doesn´t often go out in the night because she´s afraid _____ the dark.

6. I study Spanish, but I´m not very satisfied _____ my progress.

7. I've never seen so many people before. I'm astonished _____ the crowds.

8. Are you afraid _____ him?

9. I don't feel sorry _____ her because her problems are her own fault.

10. He is responsible _____ what appears in his newspaper.

11. He wasn't very keen _____ going to the cinema.

12. I'm angry _____ him for telling lies about me.

13. I think they were not interested _____ what I was saying.

14. The police are responsible _____ maintaining law and order.

15. We are short _____ workers in our factory at the moment.

16. It would be clever _____ you to study more.

17. Are you interested _____ football?

18. He always waits outside because he is frightened _____ our dog.

19. She is furious _____ him for not watering the flowers.

20. It would be stupid _____ him to go out without a coat because it is cold outside.

ADJECTIVES WITH PREPOSITIONS 1

1. She is brilliant **at** repairing things.
2. She is nice, but I don´t want to get married **to** her.
3. It's very nice **of** you to lend me your car.
4. He is married **to** his best friend's sister.
5. Why are you always so rude **to** your parents?
6. It wasn´t very polite **of** him to leave without saying thank you.
7. I can´t understand people who are cruel **to** animals.
8. I have to stop to talk to you. I'm a bit short **of** time.
9. She is excellent **at** skiing.
10. Your shoes are similar **to** mine, but they are not exactly the same.
11. We´ve got enough to eat. The fridge is full **of** food.
12. I felt sorry **for** the children because it rained every day.
13. He said he was sorry **about** the situation but there was nothing he could do.
14. She is bad **at** surfing.
15. Our house is similar **to** theirs.
16. I feel sorry **for** him because it wasn't his fault.
17. It would be clever **of** you to study more.
18. France is also very famous **for** its wine.
19. The streets were crowded **with** people.
20. She was very upset **for** not being invited to the party.

ADJECTIVES WITH PREPOSITIONS 2

1. She is very terrified **of** spiders.
2. We enjoyed our holidays, but we were disappointed **with** our hotel.
3. I was surprised **by** the way he behaved.
4. He is very fond **of** animals.
5. She doesn´t often go out in the night because she´s afraid **of** the dark.
6. I study Spanish, but I´m not very satisfied **with** my progress.
7. I've never seen so many people before. I'm astonished **by** the crowds.
8. Are you afraid **of** him?
9. I don't feel sorry **for** her because her problems are her own fault.
10. He is responsible **for** what appears in his newspaper.
11. He wasn't very keen **on** going to the cinema.
12. I'm angry **with** him for telling lies about me.
13. I think they were not interested **in** what I was saying.
14. The police are responsible **for** maintaining law and order.
15. We are short **of** workers in our factory at the moment.
16. It would be clever **of** you to study more.
17. Are you interested **in** football?
18. He always waits outside because he is frightened **of** our dog.
19. She is furious **with** him for not watering the flowers.
20. It would be stupid **of** him to go out without a coat because it is cold outside.

CONDITIONAL CLAUSES

How to form and use

Conditional clauses are also called conditional sentences or if sentences. They always have two parts, a main clause and an if-clause. These two parts are closely connected. The action in the main part can only happen if a certain condition is taking place. This condition has to be expressed in the if-clause.
Example: If he comes to my party, I will be happy.
The condition is "If he comes to my party" and the consequence of this condition is "I will be happy".

You can start a conditional clause with the main clause or the if-clause:
If I have a problem, Susan always helps me. or Susan always helps me if I have a problem.

Zero Conditional

The zero conditional is used with general statements, actions that are certainly happening and facts. We use it with things that are true. The present tense is used in both clauses.

If there **is** a problem, I **can** always **talk** to Carol.
Present Tense ------ Present Tense

First Conditional - type I

It's possible that something will happen. We use the Conditional I to talk about future situations that are realistic to happen. We use the present tense in the if-clause and the will-future in the main clause.

Colin is an intelligent boy. It is April 15th. The exam is on April 23rd. He has enough time to study for the exam - he can pass it.

If he **studies**, he **will pass** the exam on April 23rd.
Present Tense ------ Will Future

Second Conditional - type II

It's possible, but not very probable. We use the Conditional II to talk about future situations that are unreal or nearly impossible to happen. We use the past tense in the if-clause and conditional present in the main clause.

Colin didn't study. He played football. It's April 22nd. Tomorrow is the exam. It is possible, but not very probable that he will pass the exam.

If he **studied**, he **would pass** the exam.
Past Tense ------ **Conditional Present** (would + infinitive)

Third Conditional - type III

It didn't happen and it is impossible now. We use the Conditional III to talk about past situations that didn't happen. We use the past perfect tense in the if-clause and the conditional perfect in the main clause.

It's April 23rd. Colin didn't pass the exam.

If he **had studied**, he **would have passed** the exam.
Past Perfect ------ **Conditional Perfect** (would + have + 3rd form)

Using commas in conditional sentences

When the condition is at the beginning of the sentence, you have to separate it from the main clause with a comma. If the condition is at the back of the sentence, you don't use a comma.

Examples: If he comes to my party, I'll be happy. I'll be happy if he comes to my party.

CONDITIONAL CLAUSES 1

Complete with the zero or first conditional.

1. If you don't tell her the truth, she _____ angry with you! (be)
2. Soap _____ if you leave it in water. (dissolve)
3. If he rings the bell, the receptionist _____. (come)
4. If I study more, I _____ the exam. (pass)
5. Plants die if you _____ them. (not water)
6. He _____ it if she explains the situation to him. (understand)
7. Milk _____ off if you don't keep it in a cool place. (go)
8. Ask the teacher if you _____. (not understand)
9. If they offer me a job, I _____ it. (take)
10. I will have to invite Bob if I _____ Linda. (invite)
11. I _____ if you want to use the car. (not mind)
12. If Jack meets Tom, he _____ him the truth. (tell)
13. If Ella has enough money, she _____ a new car. (buy)
14. Children _____ upset if they're being bullied. (get)
15. Stamps can be good fun if you _____ collecting things. (enjoy)
16. What will Charlie do if he _____ the job? (not get)
17. It can be hard to access the web if you _____ a PC at home. (not have)
18. The heater _____ on if you press this switch. (come)
19. If you _____ to understand the text, you have to study the new words. (want)
20. If you are going out, _____ me know. (let)

CONDITIONAL CLAUSES 2

Complete with the first conditional.

1. If I _____ enough money, I will buy a new skateboard. (have)
2. If you help your mother, she _____ very happy. (be)
3. If Mary _____ in the kitchen, she will get more pocket money. (help)
4. She will be angry if you _____ the truth. (not tell)
5. You will have to walk if you _____ the bus. (miss)
6. If Tom is at home, he _____ TV. (watch)
7. The baby _____ if you are quiet. (sleep)
8. If he is in San Francisco, he _____ the Golden Gate Bridge. (see)
9. He _____ to the doctor's if he doesn't feel well tomorrow. (go)
10. If he _____ his car, he won't get much money for it. (sell)
11. I _____ to the USA if I have enough money. (travel)
12. If they _____ a car, they will drive to Italy. (buy)
13. If I work harder, I _____ the exam. (pass)
14. We _____ good marks if we don't study. (not get)
15. If he tells me the truth, I _____ glad. (be)
16. I will travel to the USA if I _____ enough money. (have)
17. If I'm offered the job, I think I _____ it. (take)
18. If she _____ up early, she will catch the bus. (get)
19. If I hear burglars, I _____ the police. (call)
20. We will go swimming if it _____ warm enough. (be)

CONDITIONAL CLAUSES 3

Complete with the second conditional.

1. If she _____ (be) hungry, she would eat something.
2. If he studied, he _____ (pass) the exam.
3. I _____ (send) you a postcard if I had your address.
4. What _____ (happen) if you didn´t go to work tomorrow?
5. She would be terribly upset if I _____ (lose) her ring.
6. Many people would be out of work if the factory _____ (close).
7. That box _____ (look) better if you painted it blue.
8. If he offered me a job, I _____ (take) it.
9. If we _____ (eat) too much, we would get fat.
10. What would you do if you _____ (be) the president of your country?
11. If he hurried, he _____ (catch) the train.
12. If he _____ (be) here, we would play cards.
13. I _____ (tell) you if you asked me.
14. If he _____ (ring) the bell, the waiter would come.
15. If you paid him well, he _____ (come).
16. We would go for a walk if it _____ (be) warmer.
17. If Mary helped in the kitchen, she _____ (get) more pocket money.
18. If I were you, I _____ (start) now.
19. He would buy that house if he _____ (have) some money.
20. If you studied harder, you _____ (write) a good test.

CONDITIONAL CLAUSES 4

Complete with the first or second conditional.

1. If he _____ (have) time, he will come.
2. If I _____ (be) you, I wouldn't do that.
3. I _____ (go) to see him if he has time.
4. If you _____ (come), you would see her.
5. If he doesn't go back now, he _____ (be) late.
6. If Charles _____ (ask) me, I would lend him my tools.
7. What will you do if you _____ (lose) the way?
8. They would be glad if the rain _____ (stop) soon.
9. If you asked us, we _____ (help) you.
10. I _____ (go) to the cinema if I had more time.
11. I will call her if I _____ (find out) her number.
12. If they _____ (be) rich, they would stay in a more expensive hotel.
13. She _____ (feel) ill if she eats so much.
14. If you helped her in the garden, she _____ (be) happy.
15. If he skis too fast, he _____ (break) his leg.
16. What will John do if he _____ (not get) the job?
17. They would get drunk if they _____ (drink) too much beer.
18. If I _____ (invite) Linda, I will have to invite Bob.
19. If I had some money, I _____ (buy) a new car.
20. You will get wet if you _____ (not take) an umbrella.

CONDITIONAL CLAUSES 5

Complete with the first or second conditional.

1. He _____ (cause) an accident if he drives too dangerously.
2. If you steal the purse, they _____ (arrest) you.
3. I _____ (tell) you if you asked me.
4. If she _____ (explain) him the situation, he will understand it.
5. I won't visit him if he _____ (be) angry.
6. He would go to the cinema if he _____ (have) more time.
7. If I find the book, I _____ (send) it.
8. If I _____ (be) at home, I will study my words.
9. They _____ (feel) better if they took their medicine.
10. If you close the door, nobody _____ (see) you.
11. If Sam _____ (have) a hammer, he will lend it to me.
12. Susan will help you if she _____ (get) more pocket money.
13. If we go to London, we _____ (see) the Tower.
14. He _____ (wash) his hands if you give him some soap.
15. If it _____ (stop) raining, we would play tennis.
16. If she had enough money, she _____ (buy) a new car.
17. I will pass the exam if I _____ (work) harder.
18. If Nelly rode her bike more carefully, she _____ (have) fewer accidents.
19. If Mr Jones _____ (watch) the news every evening, he would know more about politics.
20. If she sets the alarm clock, she _____ (not oversleep).

CONDITIONAL CLAUSES 6

Complete with the third conditional.

1. Alexander _____ to her if he had met her. (talk)
2. If I _____ at home, I would have watched the movie. (be)
3. If Jack had come to my party, I _____ with him. (dance)
4. They _____ got lost if they had read the map properly. (not have)
5. I'm sure he _____ his watch, if he had looked for it more carefully. (find)
6. If we had been in San Francisco, we _____ the Golden Gate Bridge. (pass)
7. She wouldn't have been hungry if she _____ her dinner. (eat)
8. If you _____ Harry, we would have been happy. (marry)
9. If my dad _____ his car to you, you'd have got a bargain. (sell)
10. Chloe _____ that exam easily if she had attended every lesson. (pass)
11. We _____ to the beach if it had been sunny yesterday. (go)
12. If I had told you about Chantal, you _____ me. (not believe)
13. If I _____ the doctor, she would've advised me on what to do. (ask)
14. If I had lent you my lawnmower, you _____ it. (break)
15. I _____ in if I had watched that boring show. (sleep)
16. I _____ shopping in charity shops if I had won the lottery. (not be)
17. If Zoe _____ some money, she would've handed it in. (find)
18. If Bill _____ a taxi, he would have been there by now. (take)
19. I _____ Hyde Park if I had gone on the trip to London. (visit)
20. If he _____ his book at school, he might have passed the exam. (not forget)

CONDITIONAL CLAUSES 7

Complete with the first, second or third conditional.

1. If Mr Brown _____ (sell) his car last year, he would have got more money for it.
2. If Susan takes her driving lessons regularly, she _____ (pass) her driving test.
3. If Charlie _____ (not stop) eating these green apples, he'll soon feel sick.
4. If you had told me the truth, I _____ (help) you.
5. If old Mrs White heard a strange noise, she _____ (call) the police.
6. If I _____ (have) good luck, I would have won the first prize.
7. If I _____ (be) you, I would throw away all this old junk.
8. If I got the earlier bus, I _____ (can) come home at 5 o'clock.
9. If mother _____ (make) apple pie, I'll give you a piece.
10. If Peter _____ (not leave) earlier, he would miss the bus.
11. If we missed the train, we _____ (take) a taxi.
12. If he _____ (win) a lot of money, he will fly to Paris.
13. If she is ill, she _____ (not come) to our party.
14. We _____ (play) tennis if it stopped raining.
15. I _____ (phone) her if I knew her number.
16. If they were rich, they _____ (stay) at a hotel.
17. I would have been glad if he _____ (visit) me in hospital.
18. I would pass the exam if I _____ (study) harder.
19. If the company _____ (close), it would be hard for me to find a job.
20. If we had gone to London, we _____ (see) the Tower.

CONDITIONAL CLAUSES 8

Complete with the first, second or third conditional.

1. If I _____ (eat) your chocolates, I would have felt a bit guilty.

2. She can go early on Fridays if she _____ (ask) her manager's permission.

3. If he had offered me the job, I _____ (take) it.

4. If I _____ (have) some money, I will buy a new car.

5. If you damage my car, I _____ (be) really annoyed.

6. If he _____ (drive) more carefully, he would not cause an accident.

7. We won't stay indoors if the weather _____ (be) fine.

8. She would feel better if she _____ (eat) less.

9. If the computer _____ (crash), you would lose all your unsaved work.

10. If it _____ (rain), I don't have to water the flowers.

11. She _____ (give) you an answer if you had asked her more politely.

12. If he won a lot of money, he _____ (fly) to Paris.

13. If you had asked me, I _____ (tell) you.

14. If I am at home, I _____ (watch) the movie.

15. If I _____ (be) you, I would start studying now.

16. If Jack meets Tom, he _____ (tell) him the truth.

17. His sister would have been glad if you _____ (phone) her.

18. The Millers _____ (move) to the seaside if they had had children.

19. If Jack _____ (come) to my party, I would have danced with him.

20. If she _____ (meet) him, she will talk to him.

CONDITIONAL CLAUSES 1

1. If you don't tell her the truth, she **is** angry with you!
2. Soap **dissolves** if you leave it in water.
3. If he rings the bell, the receptionist **will come**.
4. If I study more, I **will pass** the exam.
5. Plants die if you **don't water** them.
6. He **will understand** it if she explains him the situation.
7. Milk **goes** off if you don't keep it in a cool place.
8. Ask the teacher if you **don't understand**.
9. If they offer me a job, I **will take** it.
10. I will have to invite Bob if I **invite** Linda.
11. I **don't mind** if you want to use the car.
12. If Jack meets Tom, he **will tell** him the truth.
13. If Ella has enough money, she **will buy** a new car.
14. Children **get** upset if they're being bullied.
15. Stamps can be good fun if you **enjoy** collecting things.
16. What will Charlie do if he **does not get (doesn't get)** the job?
17. It can be hard to access the web if you **don't have** a PC at home.
18. The heater **comes** on if you press this switch.
19. If you **want** to understand the text, you have to study the new words.
20. If you are going out, **let** me know.

CONDITIONAL CLAUSES 2

1. If I **have** enough money, I will buy a new skateboard.
2. If you help your mother, she **will be** very happy.
3. If Mary **helps** in the kitchen, she will get more pocket money.
4. She will be angry if you **do not tell / don't tell** the truth.
5. You will have to walk if you **miss** the bus.
6. If Tom is at home, he **will watch** TV.
7. The baby **will sleep** if you are quiet.
8. If he is in San Francisco, he **will see** Golden Gate Bridge.
9. He **will go** to the doctor's if he doesn't feel well tomorrow.
10. If he **sells** his car, he won't get much money for it.
11. I **will travel** to the USA if I have enough money.
12. If they **buy** a car, they will drive to Italy.
13. If I work harder, I **will pass** the exam.
14. We **will not get / won't get** good marks if we don't study.
15. If he tells me the truth, I **will be** glad.
16. I will travel to the USA if I **have** enough money.
17. If I'm offered the job, I think I **will take** it.
18. If she **gets** up early, she will catch the bus.
19. If I hear burglars, I **will call** the police.
20. We will go swimming if it **is** warm enough.

CONDITIONAL CLAUSES 3

1. If she **was** hungry, she would eat something.
2. If he studied, he **would pass** the exam.
3. I **would send** you a postcard if I had your address.
4. What **would happen** if you didn´t go to work tomorrow?
5. She would be terribly upset if I **lost** her ring.
6. Many people would be out of work if the factory **closed**.
7. That box **would look** better if you painted it blue.
8. If he offered me a job, I **would take** it.
9. If we **ate** too much, we would get fat.
10. What would you do if you **were** the president of your country?
11. If he hurried, he **would catch** the train.
12. If he **was** here, we would play cards.
13. I **would tell** you if you asked me.
14. If he **rang** the bell, the waiter would come.
15. If you paid him well, he **would come**.
16. We would go for a walk, if it **was** warmer.
17. If Mary helped in the kitchen, she **would get** more pocket money.
18. If I were you, I **would start** now.
19. He would buy that house if he **had** some money.
20. If you studied harder, you **would write** a good test.

CONDITIONAL CLAUSES 4

1. If he **has** time, he will come.
2. If I **were** you, I wouldn't do that.
3. I **will go** to see him if he has time.
4. If you **came**, you would see her.
5. If he doesn't go back now, he **will be** late.
6. If Charles **asked** me, I would lend him my tools.
7. What will you do if you **lose** the way?
8. They would be glad if the rain **stopped** soon.
9. If you asked us, we **would help** you.
10. I **would go** to the cinema if I had more time.
11. I will call her if I **find out** her number.
12. If they **were** rich, they would stay in a more expensive hotel.
13. She **will feel** ill if she eats so much.
14. If you helped her in the garden, she **would be** happy.
15. If he skis too fast, he **will break** his leg.
16. What will John do if he **does not get** the job?
17. They would get drunk if they **drank** too much beer.
18. If I **invite** Linda, I will have to invite Bob.
19. If I had some money, I **would buy** a new car.
20. You will get wet if you **don't take** an umbrella.

CONDITIONAL CLAUSES 5

1. He **will cause** an accident if he drives too dangerously.
2. If you steal the purse, they **will arrest** you.
3. I **would tell** you if you asked me.
4. If she **explains** him the situation, he will understand it.
5. I won't visit him if he **is** angry.
6. He would go to the cinema if he **had** more time.
7. If I find the book, I **will send** it.
8. If I **am** at home, I will study my words.
9. They **would feel** better if they took their medicine.
10. If you close the door, nobody **will see** you.
11. If Sam **has** a hammer, he will lend it to me.
12. Susan will help you if she **gets** more pocket money.
13. If we go to London, we **will see** the Tower.
14. He **will wash** his hands if you give him some soap.
15. If it **stopped** raining, we would play tennis.
16. If she had enough money, she **would buy** a new car.
17. I will pass the exam if I **work** harder.
18. If Nelly rode her bike more carefully, she **would have** fewer accidents.
19. If Mr Jones **watched** the news every evening, he would know more about politics.
20. If she sets the alarm clock, she **will not oversleep**.

CONDITIONAL CLAUSES 6

1. Alexander **would have talked** to her if he had met her.
2. If I **had been** at home, I would have watched the movie.
3. If Jack had come to my party, I **would have danced** with him.
4. They **wouldn't have** got lost if they had read the map properly.
5. I'm sure he **would have found** his watch, if he had looked for it more carefully.
6. If we had been in San Francisco, we **would have passed** the Golden Gate Bridge.
7. She wouldn't have been hungry if she **had eaten** her dinner.
8. If you **had married** Harry, we would have been happy.
9. If my dad **had sold** his car to you, you'd have got a bargain.
10. Chloe **would have passed** that exam easily if she had attended every lesson.
11. We **would've gone** to the beach if it had been sunny yesterday.
12. If I had told you about Chantal, you **wouldn't have believed** me.
13. If I **had asked** the doctor, she would've advised me on what to do.
14. If I had lent you my lawnmower, you **would have broken** it.
15. I **would have slept** in if I had watched that boring show.
16. I **wouldn't have been** shopping in charity shops if I had won the lottery.
17. If Zoe **had found** some money, she would've handed it in.
18. If Bill **had taken** a taxi, he would have been there by now.
19. I **would've visited** Hyde Park if I had gone on the trip to London.
20. If he **hadn't forgotten** his book at school, he might have passed the exam.

CONDITIONAL CLAUSES 7

1. If Mr Brown **had sold** his car last year, he would have got more money for it.
2. If Susan takes her driving lessons regularly, she **will pass** her driving test.
3. If Charlie **does not stop** eating these green apples, he'll soon feel sick.
4. If you had told me the truth, I **would have helped** you.
5. If old Mrs White heard a strange noise, she **would call** the police.
6. If I **had had** good luck, I would have won the first prize.
7. If I **were / was** you, I would throw away all this old junk.
8. If I got the earlier bus, I **would be able to / could** come home at 5 o'clock.
9. If mother **makes** apple pie, I'll give you a piece.
10. If Peter **did not leave** earlier, he would miss the bus.
11. If we missed the train, we **would take** a taxi.
12. If he **wins** a lot of money, he will fly to Paris.
13. If she is ill, she **will not come** to our party.
14. We **would play** tennis if it stopped raining.
15. I **would phone** her if I knew her number.
16. If they were rich, they **would stay** at a hotel.
17. I would have been glad if he **had visited** me in hospital.
18. I would pass the exam if I **studied** harder.
19. If the company **closed**, it would be hard for me to find a job.
20. If we had gone to London, we **would have seen** the Tower.

CONDITIONAL CLAUSES 8

1. If I **had eaten** your chocolates, I would have felt a bit guilty.
2. She can go early on Fridays if she **asks** her manager's permission.
3. If he had offered me the job, I **would have taken** it.
4. If I **have** some money, I will buy a new car.
5. If you damage my car, I **will be** really annoyed.
6. If he **drove** more carefully, he would not cause an accident.
7. We won't stay indoors if the weather **is** fine.
8. She would feel better if she **ate** less.
9. If the computer **crashed**, you would lose all your unsaved work.
10. If it **rains**, I don't have to water the flowers.
11. She **would have given** you an answer if you had asked her more politely.
12. If he won a lot of money, he **would fly** to Paris.
13. If you had asked me, I **would have told** you.
14. If I am at home, I **will watch** the movie.
15. If I **was / were** you, I would start studying now.
16. If Jack meets Tom, he **will tell** him the truth.
17. His sister would have been glad if you **had phoned** her.
18. The Millers **would have moved** to the seaside if they had had children.
19. If Jack **had come** to my party, I would have danced with him.
20. If she **meets** him, she will talk to him.

FUTURE TENSES

There are four different ways in English to talk about the future. You can use the simple future, the going to - future, the present progressive and the present pimple to write or talk about future actions. There is often only a little difference between the future tenses, especially between the going to - future and the present progressive. It also depends on the country and region and on the communication what future tense is used. In written English the simple future is usually used while in spoken English we use the going to - future more often.

The simple future (will – future) **is used:**

- to talk about future actions, we can't influence or control.
- to foretell future actions or to express hopes, expectations, fears, offers, promises, refusals....
  Key words: I'm sure, I believe, I expect, I hope, I suppose, I think, I'm afraid, I wonder, I fear, I worry, I promise, I guess or perhaps, possibly, surely, probably, maybe

- with I / we for spontaneous reactions or making promises
  I shall is sometimes used instead of I will.

The going to - future **is used:**

- to talk about future things you intend to do, plan or decided to do
  Examples:
  Did you know that Sarah is in hospital? - No, I didn't. I'll visit her this afternoon. (spontaneous reaction »»» will - future)
  Yes, I'm going to visit her next month. (planned action »»» going to - future)
- to foretell future actions for which we have proofs that they are going to happen.

The present progressive **is used:**

- to talk about future things that are fixed, planned or definitely decided
  The speaker must refer to the future and not to the present.
  Examples: I am visiting my grandparents tomorrow.
                What are you doing next Friday?

The present simple **is used:**

- to talk about times of arrivals and departures of traffic and times of events.
  Examples: The train leaves at 10.20.
                The bus goes at 8.30.
                When does the concert begin?

FUTURE TENSES 1

Fill in **going to** or **the simple future tense** (=will future).

1. I _____ them tomorrow evening. (meet)
2. _____ him for help? (you ask)
3. Susan _____ the bathroom next weekend. (paint)
4. I think he _____ her name. (find out)
5. I _____ a walk in the garden this evening. (take)
6. Let's hope that the wind _____ away the clouds. (blow)
7. Mary _____ a good mark because she has studied hard. (get)
8. Are you sure, you _____ in a tent in your holidays? (sleep)
9. Peter _____ his new bike in the park. (ride)
10. I hope Jane _____ me to her party. (invite)
11. I _____ dad's car tomorrow afternoon. (wash)
12. Mum thinks dad _____ home early tonight. (come)
13. It _____ very cold in the mountains. Take a sweater with you. (probably be)
14. We _____ our bikes in the park. Can you come with us? (ride)
15. I think Susan _____ in love with Mike. (fall)
16. It's late. I hope we _____ the bus. (not miss)
17. _____ the new words this time, Peter? (you study)
18. Next summer we _____ at a campsite near a lake. (probably stay)
19. We _____ to Scotland this summer. (go)
20. I promise, I _____ you tomorrow. (phone)
21. Maybe he _____ any time next weekend. (not have)
22. She _____ a baby next April. (have)
23. I hope the train _____ delayed. (not be)
24. They _____ the exam. (probably pass)
25. The sky is cloudy and grey. It _____. (rain)

FUTURE TENSES 2

Fill in the correct future tense – **simple future, going to future** or **present progressive**.

1. They _____ to New York tomorrow morning. (drive)
2. I hope the weather _____ nice. (be)
3. John _____ to his new CD this evening. (listen)
4. I offered him this job. I think he _____ it. (take)
5. Jane and Sue _____ a present for mum's birthday. (buy)
6. I hope you _____ me with the dishes, Julie. (help)
7. I promise I _____ your secret to anyone. (not tell)
8. Take your umbrella with you. It _____ (rain).
9. They _____ cards this evening. (play)
10. When the weather is fine, we _____ a picnic in our garden. (probably have)
11. I think the police _____ the burglars. (arrest)
12. They _____ to Seattle next summer holidays. (fly)
13. I _____ 50 people to the party and I hope everyone _____. (invite / come)
14. That exercise looks difficult. I _____ you. (help)
15. _____ to the football match? (he go)
16. Are you sure they _____ the match? (win)
17. It _____ very cold in the mountains. Take a sweater with you. (probably be)
18. He _____ tomorrow. (not leave)
19. We think he _____ home late in the night. (come)
20. It's my birthday next Friday. Mum _____ a cake. (bake)

FUTURE TENSES 1

1. I **am going to meet** them tomorrow evening.
2. **Are you going to ask** him for help?
3. Susan **is going to paint** the bathroom next weekend.
4. I think he **will find out** her name.
5. I **am going to take** a walk in the garden this evening.
6. Let's hope that the wind **will blow** away the clouds.
7. Mary **is going to get** a good mark because she has studied hard.
8. Are you sure, you **will sleep** in a tent in your holidays?
9. Peter **is going to ride** his new bike in the park.
10. I hope Jane **will invite** me to her party.
11. I **am going to wash** dad's car tomorrow afternoon.
12. Mum thinks dad **will come** home early tonight. (come)
13. It **will probably be** very cold in the mountains. Take a sweater with you.
14. We **are going to ride** our bikes in the park. Can you come with us?
15. I think Susan **will fall** in love with Mike.
16. It's late. I hope we **will not miss / won't miss** the bus.
17. **Are you going to study** the new words this time, Peter?
18. Next summer we **will probably stay** at a campsite near a lake.
19. We **are going to go** to Scotland this summer.
20. I promise, I **will phone** you tomorrow.
21. Maybe he **will not have / won't have** any time next weekend.
22. She **is going to have** a baby next April.
23. I hope the train **will not be / won't be** delayed.
24. They **will probably pass** the exam.
25. The sky is cloudy and grey. It **is going to rain**.

FUTURE TENSES 2

1. They **are driving** to New York tomorrow morning.
2. I hope the weather **will be** nice.
3. John **is going to listen** to his new CD this evening.
4. I offered him this job. I think he **will take** it.
5. Jane and Sue **are going to buy** a present for mum's birthday.
6. I hope you **will help** me with the dishes, Julie.
7. I promise I **will not tell** your secret to anyone.
8. Take your umbrella with you. It **is going to rain**.
9. They **are going to play / are playing** cards this evening.
10. When the weather is fine, we **will probably have** a picnic in our garden.
11. I think the police **will arrest** the burglars.
12. They **are flying / are going to fly** to Seattle next summer holidays.
13. I **am inviting** (invite) 50 people to the party, and I hope everyone **will come**.
14. That exercise looks difficult. I **will help** you.
15. **Is he going** to the football match?
16. Are you sure they **will win** the match?
17. It **will probably be** very cold in the mountains. Take a sweater with you.
18. He **is not leaving / isn't leaving** tomorrow.
19. We think he **will come** home late in the night.
20. It's my birthday next Friday. Mum **is going to bake** a cake.

THE PASSIVE VOICE

How the passive is formed:

SUBJECT	FORM OF TO BE + 3rd FORM	ADVERB, ...
The room	is cleaned	every day.
They	are sold	as pets.
A lot of guests	are invited	to a party.

Put an active sentence into a passive one:

	Subject	Verb	Object		
Active:	Bats	eat	insects.		
Passive:	Insects	are eaten	by	bats.	
	Subject	Verb	by	Agent	

	Subject	Verb	Object		
Active:	Tom	saw	the burglars		
Passive:	The burglars	were seen	by	Tom	
	Subject	Verb	by	Agent	

Subject of the active sentence → **Agent** of the passive sentence
Object of the active sentence → **Subject** of the passive sentence

Tenses:

Tense	Active	Passive (form of to be + 3rd form)
Present tense	invite / see	am / is / are invited / seen
Past tense	invited / saw	was / were invited / seen
Future tense	will invite / see	will be invited / seen
Present perfect tense	have / has invited / seen	have / has been invited / seen
Past perfect tense	had invited / seen	had been invited / seen

PASSIVE VOICE 1

Fill in the passive form of the verbs in brackets. Use the present simple.

1. This computer _____ in the USA. (make)
2. Her dog _____ Rover. (call)
3. Lots of new cars _____ by train. (transport)
4. Our neighbours' house _____ every year. (paint)
5. Jim _____ well by the new company owners. (not pay)
6. Today many insects _____ by poison. (kill)
7. Baby seals _____ on dangerous beaches. (bear)
8. English _____ in many parts of the world. (speak)
9. This theme park _____ very often on weekdays. (not visit)
10. These watches _____ in Switzerland. (make)
11. This helicopter _____ for taking people to hospital. (use)
12. All her toys _____ in a big box. (keep)
13. The buses _____ every week. (clean)
14. The post _____ twice a day. (collect)
15. Foreign vegetables _____ on this market. (not sell)
16. Whales _____ in order to make cosmetics. (hunt)
17. Excellent tea _____ by India and Sri Lanka. (export)
18. The corridors _____ on weekends. (not clean)
19. Every year a big Christmas tree _____ up in our town. (put)
20. The tennis court next to our house _____ very often. (not use)

PASSIVE VOICE 2

Fill in the passive form of the verbs in brackets. Use the present or past simple.

1. He _____ (offer) a new job last week.
2. The bridge _____ (blow off) yesterday.
3. This novel _____ (write) by Hemingway.
4. Flies _____ (catch) by spiders.
5. All the trees _____ (cut) down yesterday.
6. We _____ (tell) to go home now.
7. Their purse _____ (steal) in the disco last night.
8. Rain _____ (hold) up by fog.
9. He _____ (throw) out of the bar a week ago.
10. Pigs _____ (use) to find truffles.
11. The old theatre _____ (reopen) last Friday.
12. She _____ (ask) about the accident by the police yesterday.
13. A lot of food _____ (throw) away every day.
14. Mice _____ (catch) by cats.
15. I _____ (usually invited) to her parties.
16. Policemen _____ (often ask) for the way.
17. They _____ (teach) French last term.
18. The lawn _____ (cut) once a week.
19. The tickets _____ (buy) by her last week.
20. The shoes _____ (clean) every morning.

PASSIVE VOICE 3

Fill in the passive form of the verbs in brackets. Use the past simple.

1. Many pictures _____ (paint) by Picasso.
2. Sue _____ (take) to school by her father.
3. His car _____ (damage) in an accident.
4. Football _____ first _____ (play) in England.
5. Some roads _____ (destroy) by an earthquake.
6. The window _____ (break) by a ball.
7. That cottage _____ (build) by a famous architect.
8. One person _____ (find) by the helicopter rescue team.
9. Our car _____ (sell) yesterday.
10. The key _____ (forget) by an old man.
11. The accident _____ (see) by two girls.
12. The bank _____ (rob) three days ago.
13. The engine _____ (invent) by George Stevenson.
14. The lives of many people _____ (save) by his dog.
15. Jack _____ (invite) to their party.
16. The potatoes _____ (load) onto lorries.
17. The robbers _____ (arrest) by the police.
18. The parcel _____ (send) by mail.
19. The book and the pencil _____ (leave) behind.
20. All the magazines _____ (sell) yesterday.

PASSIVE VOICE 4

Put the following sentences into the passive voice.

1. Nelly ate all the cake.
   _____

2. They opened the windows.
   _____

3. We bought this present.
   _____

4. He sold his flat last summer.
   _____

5. We sang English songs.
   _____

6. My friends saw Marry in the park.
   _____

7. The children found the key.
   _____

8. The police arrested the burglars.
   _____

Fill in the passive form of the verbs in brackets. Use the past tense.

Three days ago, Nepal _____ (rock) by a very strong earthquake. About two hundred people _____ (kill) and thousands _____ (take) to the local hospitals. They _____ (treat) for shock and their injuries _____ (care for). A lot of houses _____ (destroy). The city hall _____ also _____ (damage).

PASSIVE VOICE 5

Put the sentences into the passive voice.

1. They built these houses in 1902.
___

2. She bakes a cake every Sunday.
___

3. He broke the vase yesterday.
___

4. I clean the shoes every Friday.
___

5. We wrote the exercise an hour ago.
___

6. They use this road very often.
___

7. Thieves stole his car.
___

8. They cancelled all the flights.
___

9. Brian told the truth.
___

10. She always loads the dishwasher.
___

11. He sometimes does the shopping.
___

12. The ambulance took Peter to hospital.

PASSIVE VOICE 6

Put the following sentences into the passive voice.

1. My grandfather built this house.
   _____

2. Carol always waters the flowers.
   _____

3. The boys did the homework.
   _____

4. Susan wrote this email.
   _____

5. George has opened a hotel.
   _____

6. Peter solved this problem.
   _____

7. An electric fault caused the fire.
   _____

8. Her mother will clean the room.
   _____

9. The police arrested three men.
   _____

10. We haven't seen her for weeks.
    _____

11. They will pull down the old building.
    _____

12. Helen found the key.

PASSIVE VOICE 7

Complete the sentences with the passive forms of the verbs. Use the tense in brackets.

1. English _____ (speak) all over the world. (Present tense)

2. This quarrel _____ (forget) in a few years' time. (Future tense)

3. My pencil case _____ (steal). (Present perfect)

4. We have _____ (never / beat) at badminton. (Present perfect)

5. This shirt _____ (make) in France. (Past tense)

6. Our dogs _____ (keep) in the house. (Present tense)

7. Her new book _____ (publish) next month. (Future tense)

8. Milk _____ (use) to make butter and cheese. (Present tense)

9. They _____ (take) to school. (Past tense)

10. Not a sound _____ (hear). (Past tense)

11. Some juice _____ (spill) on the carpet. (Present perfect)

12. The thieves _____ (arrest) by the police. (Past tense)

13. The homework _____ (correct) by the teacher. (Future tense)

14. Her ring _____ (find) under the bed. (Past tense)

15. I _____ (offer) an interesting job. (Past tense)

16. My brother _____ (just beat) in the race. (Present perfect)

17. He _____ (tell) to wait outside. (Past tense)

18. The fire brigade _____ (phone) soon after the fire broke out. (Past perfect)

19. The email _____ (answer) tomorrow. (Future tense)

20. The best cookies _____ (sell) here. (Present tense)

PASSIVE VOICE 1

1. This computer **is made** in the USA.
2. Her dog **is called** Rover.
3. Lots of new cars **are transported** by train.
4. Our neighbours' house **is painted** every year.
5. Jim **isn't paid** well by the new company owners.
6. Today many insects **are killed** by poison.
7. Baby seals **are born** on dangerous beaches.
8. English **is spoken** in many parts of the world.
9. This theme park **isn't visited** very often on weekdays.
10. These watches **are made** in Switzerland.
11. This helicopter **is used** for taking people to hospital.
12. All her toys **are kept** in a big box.
13. The buses **are cleaned** every week.
14. The post **is collected** twice a day.
15. Foreign vegetables **aren't sold** on this market.
16. Whales **are hunted** in order to make cosmetics.
17. Excellent tea **is exported** by India and Sri Lanka.
18. The corridors **aren't cleaned** on weekends.
19. Every year a big Christmas tree **is put** up in our town.
20. The tennis court next to our house **isn't used** very often.

PASSIVE VOICE 2

1. He **was offered** (offer) a new job last week.
2. The bridge **was blown off** (blow off) yesterday.
3. This novel **was written** (write) by Hemingway.
4. Flies **are caught** (catch) by spiders.
5. All the trees **were cut** (cut) down yesterday.
6. We **are told** (tell) to go home now.
7. Their purse **was stolen** (steal) in the disco last night.
8. Rain **is held** (hold) up by fog.
9. He **was thrown** (throw) out of the bar a week ago.
10. Pigs **are used** (use) to find truffles.
11. The old theatre **was reopened** (reopen) last Friday.
12. She **was asked** (ask) about the accident by the police yesterday.
13. A lot of food **is thrown** (throw) away every day.
14. Mice **are caught** (catch) by cats.
15. I **am usually invited** to her parties.
16. Policemen **are often asked** (often ask) for the way.
17. They **were taught** (teach) French last term.
18. The lawn **is cut** (cut) once a week.
19. The tickets **were bought** by her last week.
20. The shoes **are cleaned** every morning.

PASSIVE VOICE 3

1. Many pictures **were painted** by Picasso.
2. Sue **was taken** to school by her father.
3. His car **was damaged** in an accident.
4. Football **was** first **played** in England.
5. Some roads **were destroyed** by an earthquake.
6. The window **was broken** by a ball.
7. That cottage **was built** by a famous architect.
8. One person **was found** by the helicopter rescue team.
9. Our car **was sold** yesterday.
10. The key **was forgotten** by an old man.
11. The accident **was seen** by two girls.
12. The bank **was robbed** three days ago.
13. The engine **was invented** by George Stevenson.
14. The lives of many people **were saved** by his dog.
15. Jack **was invited** to their party.
16. The potatoes **were loaded** onto lorries.
17. The robbers **were arrested** by the police.
18. The parcel **was sent** by mail.
19. The book and the pencil **were left** behind.
20. All the magazines **were sold** yesterday.

PASSIVE VOICE 4

1. All the cake was eaten by Nelly.
2. The windows were opened by them.
3. This present was bought by us.
4. His flat was sold last summer.
5. English songs were sung by us.
6. Mary was seen in the park by my friends.
7. The key was found by the children.
8. The burglars were arrested by the police.

Three days ago, Nepal **was rocked** by a very strong earthquake. About two hundred people **were killed** and thousands **were taken** to the local hospitals. They **were treated** for shock and their injuries **were cared for** (care for). A lot of houses **were destroyed**. The city hall **was** also **damaged** (damage).

PASSIVE VOICE 5

1. These houses **were built** by them in 1902.
2. A cake **is baked** by her every Sunday.
3. The vase **was broken** by him yesterday.
4. The shoes **are cleaned** by me every Friday.
5. The exercise **was written** by us an hour ago.
6. This road **is used** by them very often.
7. His car **was stolen** by thieves.
8. All the flights **were cancelled** by them.
9. The truth **was told** by Brian.
10. The dishwasher **is** always **loaded** by her.
11. The shopping **is** sometimes **done** by him.
12. Peter **was taken** to hospital by the ambulance.

Passive voice 6

1. This house **was built** by my grandfather.
2. The flowers **are always watered** by Carol.
3. The homework **was done** by the boys.
4. This email **was written** by Susan.
5. A hotel **has been opened** by George.
6. This problem **was solved** by Peter.
7. The fire **was caused** by an electric fault.
8. The room **will be cleaned** by her mother.
9. Three men **were arrested** by the police.
10. She **hasn't been seen** by us for weeks.
11. The old building **will be pulled** down by them.
12. The key **was found** by Helen.

PASSIVE VOICE 7

1. English **is spoken** all over the world.
2. This quarrel **will be forgotten** in a few years' time.
3. My pencil case **has been stolen**.
4. We have **never been beaten** at badminton.
5. This shirt **was made** in France.
6. Our dogs **are kept** in the house.
7. Her new book **will be published** next month.
8. Milk **is used** to make butter and cheese.
9. They **were taken** to school.
10. Not a sound **was heard**.
11. Some juice **has been spilt** on the carpet.
12. The thieves **were arrested** by the police.
13. The homework **will be corrected** by the teacher.
14. Her ring **was found** under the bed.
15. I **was offered** an interesting job.
16. My brother **has just been beaten** in the race.
17. He **was told** to wait outside.
18. The fire brigade **had been phoned** soon after the fire broke out.
19. The email **will be answered** tomorrow.
20. The best cookies **are sold** here.

REPORTED SPEECH

1. If the reporting verb is in the **past form** (said, told...), you must change the tense.

Direct speech	Indirect speech	Direct Speech	Indirect speech
Present simple	Past simple	go	went
Present progressive	Past progressive	am/is/are going	was/were going
Past simple	Past perfect	went	had gone
Past progressive	Past perfect progressive	was/were going	had been going
Present perfect simple	Past perfect	has/have gone	had gone
Present perfect progressive	Past perfect progressive	has/have been going	had been going
Future	Conditional I	will go	would go

Example: Peter said, "Carol **is** a nice girl." Peter said (that) Carol **was** a nice girl.

Don't change these verbs: **might, could, would, should**
Example: He said, "I might arrive late." He said (that) he might arrive late.

In some cases, you don't need to change the tense, e.g. if statements are still true or if you use a general statement. But changing tenses is never wrong.
John said," My sister works for a law firm." John said that his sister works / worked for a law firm.
Sandra said," I like vanilla ice cream." Sandra said that she likes / liked vanilla ice cream.

2. When you form the reported speech, you must pay attention that the **pronouns** refer to the correct person.

   Examples: Susan said, "My parents are clever scientists."
   Susan said (that) her parents were clever scientists.

   Tom said, "I like PE best."
   Tom said (that) he liked PE best.

   They said, "We went swimming with our friends."
   They said (that) they had gone swimming with their friend.

   Betty said, "Sam told me the truth."
   Betty said (that) Sam had told her the truth.

	Direct speech	Indirect speech
She said	I - my - me	she - her - her
He said	I - my - me	he - his - him
They said	they - their - them	we - our - us

You and your:

They told her / him / me / them / us, "George loves **you**."
They told her / him / me / them / us (that) George loved her / him / me / them / us.

They told her / him / me / them / us, "George loves **your** sister."
They told her / him / me / them / us (that) George loved her / his / my / their / our sister.

They told her / him / me / them / us, "**You** are clever."
They told her / him / me / them / us (that) she / he / I / they / we was / were clever.

3. Expressions of time and place often may need to be changed.

We do not need to change **time words** if we report something around the same time, but we need to change them if we report something at a different time.
We do not need to change **place words** if we are in the same place, but we need to change them when we are in a different place.

		Direct speech	Indirect speech
Time		now	then
		today	that day
		yesterday	the day before
		tomorrow	the next / following day
		last week, month...	the previous week, month...
		next week, month...	the following week, month...
Place		here	there
		this	that
		these	those

Example: She said, "I have already seen Carol **today**."
She said (that) she had already seen Carol **that day**.

4. Reported Questions

If there is a question word, we keep it.

Examples:
They asked me, "Where is the next supermarket?" They asked me where the next supermarket was.
She asked them, "How often do you play golf?" She asked them how often they played golf.

If there is no question word, we start the reported speech with if or whether.

Examples:
She asked me, "Do you like some tea?" She asked me if/whether I liked some tea.
We asked them, "Did she arrive in time?" We asked them if/whether she had arrived in time.

5. Reported Requests

If someone asks you in a polite way, use (not) to + infinitive

Examples:
He asked her, "Could you close the door, please?" He asked her to close the door.
She asked them, "Help me, please." She asked them to help her.

6. Reported Commands

If someone doesn't ask you politely or gives you an order, use (not) to + infinitive.

Examples:
He told me, "Be quiet!" He told me to be quiet.
She told us, "Don't stay up too late!" She told us not to stay up too late.

REPORTED SPEECH 1

Put the following sentences into the reported speech.

1. The boys said, "We are on time."
   _____

2. Sue said, "He is studying for his exam."
   _____

3. Bill said, "I'm going to answer the phone."
   _____

4. The girls said, "We're not doing our homework now."
   _____

5. Mother said, "You can help me with the dishes."
   _____

6. He said, "I meet him every Friday."
   _____

7. Jim told me, "I leave tonight."
   _____

8. He said, "I'm watching TV."
   _____

9. She told them, "My mother likes roast beef."
   _____

10. The patients said, "We buy a newspaper every day."
    _____

11. They told me, "We are flying to New York."
    _____

12. Mark said, "She likes something to drink."
    _____

REPORTED SPEECH 2

1. Mr Brown said, "I was watching TV last night."

    Mr Brown said (that) _____.

2. Sandy explained, "I saw an accident at the corner of High Street."

    Sandy explained (that) _____.

3. Bob said, "We had a wonderful time at Peter's party."

    Bob said (that) _____.

4. The farmer said, "I didn't see her."

    The farmer said (that) _____.

5. Will and Tim said, "We were very happy about the present."

    Will and Tim said (that) _____.

6. Mr Jones said, "As a young boy I collected stickers."

    Mr Jones said (that) _____.

7. Peter reported, "We played a lot of tennis last year."

    Peter reported (that) _____.

8. Mother said, "I had a headache."

    Mother said (that) _____.

9. The Clarks told us, "We drove to Athens last summer."

    The Clarks told us (that) _____.

10. Helen said, "I was watching the late-night show."

    Helen said (that) _____.

11. Peter said, "They were interested in travelling to other countries."

    Peter said (that) _____.

12. Mr Cooper said, "I took my medicine regularly."

    Mr Cooper said (that) _____.

13. Mrs Miller said, "I didn't feel better."

    Mrs Miller said (that) _____.

14. Sarah said, "My father took me to school every day."

    Sarah said (that) _____.

15. He said to the reporters, "I was a farmer in Cornwall."

    He said to the reporters (that) _____.

REPORTED SPEECH 3

Put the following sentences into the reported speech.

1. She said, "The sandwich tastes good."

   _____

2. She said, "I went to the cinema."

   _____

3. Mark said, "I like coffee with milk."

   _____

4. She said, "Helen often gets good marks."

   _____

5. The teacher said, "Tim wrote a nice text."

   _____

6. She said, "He is ill today."

   _____

7. They said, "The children like fish and chips."

   _____

8. Emily said, "I have a headache."

   _____

9. He said, "I moved there last summer."

   _____

10. He said, "I repaired my bike."

    _____

11. They said, "Mrs Parker wasn't at home."

    _____

12. They told us, "The boys have listened to music since 10 o'clock."

REPORTED SPEECH 4

Put the following sentences into the reported speech.

1. Jessica reported, "I saw the accident at the corner of High Street."
   _____

2. Bob said, "We had a wonderful time at Peter's party."
   _____

3. Harry and Tim said, "We were very happy about the present."
   _____

4. Thomas told us, "I played a lot of tennis last year."
   _____

5. Helen said, "I'm watching the late-night show."
   _____

6. They said, "We studied the new words."
   _____

7. The girls said, "The test was easy."
   _____

8. The boys said, "We are angry."
   _____

9. She said, "The girls ate some toast and drank some tea."
   _____

10. He told us, "I will do my homework."
    _____

11. They told us, "Thieves stole two paintings."
    _____

12. Sarah said, "My father takes me to school every day."
    _____

REPORTED SPEECH 5

Put the following sentences into the reported speech.

1. Liam said, "I will arrive in time."
   _____

2. She said, "I met Carol last Friday."
   _____

3. They said, "We went to bed early yesterday."
   _____

4. She said, "I've never been in Japan."
   _____

5. They told me, "We were playing in the park."
   _____

6. Tom told me, "I meet my friends on the way to school."
   _____

7. He told us, "I haven't met her before."
   _____

8. The boys said, "We'll be at home by 7."
   _____

9. Sandra said, "I did some shopping last week."
   _____

10. Helen said, "The tickets for the show are very expensive."
    _____

11. She said, "I'm reading."
    _____

12. Bill said, "I've played tennis for years."

REPORTED SPEECH 6

Put the following sentences into the reported speech.

1. He asked me, "Do you know the man crossing the road?"

2. She asked them, "When did he go to bed yesterday?"

3. The children said, "We are waiting for our mother."

4. They asked her, "Have you met him before?"

5. They told him, "Shut the door!"

6. She asked them, "How long has it been raining?"

7. He said, "They took me to the next hospital."

8. They asked, "Who is standing next to Mike?"

9. She asked me, "Are you going out tonight?"

10. She told him, "Give me back my camera!"

11. They said, "We met him at the snack bar."

12. He asked her, "Have you ever been here before?"

REPORTED SPEECH 7

Put the following sentences into the reported speech.

1. They asked us, "Are you going to the cinema this week?"
   _____

2. He asked her, "How long have you played football?"
   _____

3. She asked me, "Where are you going?"
   _____

4. They told her, "Do not lie to us!"
   _____

5. He asked them, "Did you work hard yesterday?"
   _____

6. They asked him, "When did you get up this morning?"
   _____

7. They asked me, "How do you feel today?"
   _____

8. She told them, "Stop talking!"
   _____

9. She asked her, "Were you busy last week?"
   _____

10. He asked me, "Which animal are you afraid of?"
    _____

11. They told us, "Listen to the radio!"
    _____

12. She asked him, "Why did your car break down?"

REPORTED SPEECH 1

1. The boys said (that) **they were** on time.
2. Sue said (that) he **was studying** for his exam.
3. Bill said (that) **he was going** to answer the phone.
4. The girls said (that) they **were not doing their** homework **then**.
5. Mother said (that) I **could help her** with the dishes.
6. He said (that) **he met** him every Friday.
7. Jim told me (that**) he left that night**.
8. He said (that) **he was watching** TV.
9. She told them (that) **her** mother **liked (likes)** roast beef. – information is still true
10. The patients said (that) **they bought** a newspaper every day.
11. They told me (that) **they were flying** to New York.
12. Mark said (that) she **liked** something to drink.

REPORTED SPEECH 2

1. Mr Brown said (that) **he had been watching TV the night before.**
2. Sandy explained (that) **she had seen an accident at the corner of High Street.**
3. Bob said (that) **they had had a wonderful time at Peter's party.**
4. The farmer said (that) **he hadn't seen her.**
5. Will and Tim said (that) **they had been very happy about the present.**
6. Mr Jones said (that) **as a young boy he had collected stickers.**
7. Peter reported (that) **they had played a lot of tennis the year before.**
8. Mother said (that) **she had had a headache.**
9. The Clarks told us (that) **they had driven to Athens the summer before.**
10. Helen said (that) **she had been watching the late-night show.**
11. Peter said (that) **they had been interested in travelling to other countries.**
12. Mr Cooper said (that) **he had taken his medicine regularly.**
13. Mrs Miller said (that) **she hadn't felt better.**
14. Sarah said (that) **her father had taken her to school.**
15. He said to the reporters (that) **he had been a farmer in Cornwall.**

REPORTED SPEECH 3

1. She said (that) the sandwich **tasted** good.
2. She said (that) **she had gone** to the cinema.
3. Mark said (that) **he liked (likes)** coffee with milk.
4. She said (that) Helen often **got** good marks.
5. The teacher said (that) Tim **had written** a nice text.
6. She said (that) he **was** ill **that day**.
7. They said (that) the children **liked (like)** fish and chips.
8. Emily said (that) **she had** a headache.
9. He said (that) **he had moved** there the summer before / **he moved** there last summer.
10. He said (that) **he had repaired his** bike.
11. They said (that) Mrs Parker **had not (hadn't) been** at home.
12. They told us (that) the boys **had listened** to music since 10 o'clock.

REPORTED SPEECH 4

1. Jessica reported (that) she **had seen** the accident at the corner of High Street.
2. Bob said (that) they **had had** a wonderful time at Peter's party.
3. Harry and Tim said (that) they **had been** very happy about the present.
4. Thomas told us (that) he **had played** a lot of tennis last year.
5. Helen said (that) she **was watching** the late-night show.
6. They said (that) **they had studied** the new words.
7. The girls said (that) the test **had been** easy.
8. The boys said (that) **they were** angry.
9. She said (that) the girls **had eaten** some toast and **had drunk** some tea.
10. He told us (that) **he would do his** homework.
11. They told us (that) thieves **had stolen** two paintings.
12. Sarah said (that) her father **took** her to school every day.

REPORTED SPEECH 5

1. Liam said (that) he **would arrive** in time.
2. She said (that) **she had met** Carol **the Friday before**.
3. They said (that) **they had gone** to bed early **the day before**.
4. She said (that) **she had** never **been** in Japan.
5. They told me (that) **they had been** playing in the park.
6. Tom told me (that) he **met his** friends on the way to school.
7. He told us (that) **he hadn't met** her before.
8. The boys said (that) **they would be** at home by 7.
9. Sandra said (that) **she had done** some shopping **the week before**.
10. Helen said (that) the tickets for the show **were** very expensive.
11. She said (that) **she was reading**.
12. Bill said (that) **he had played** tennis for years.

REPORTED SPEECH 6

1. He asked me **if I knew** the man crossing the road.
2. She asked them **when he had gone** to bed **the day before**.
3. The children said (that) **they were waiting** for **their** mother.
4. They asked her **if she had met** him before.
5. They told him **to shut** the door.
6. She asked them **how long it had been raining**.
7. He said (that) they **had taken him** to the next hospital.
8. They asked **who was standing** next to Mike.
9. She asked me **if I was going out that night**.
10. She told him **to give her** back **her** camera.
11. They said (that) **they had met** him at the snack bar.
12. He asked her **if she had ever been there** before.

REPORTED SPEECH 7

1. They asked us **if we were going** to the cinema **that** week.
2. He asked her **how long she had played** volleyball.
3. She asked me **where I was going**.
4. They told her **not to lie to them**.
5. He asked them **if they had worked** hard **the day before**.
6. They asked him **when he had got (gotten) up that** morning.
7. They asked me **how I felt that day**.
8. She told them **to stop** talking.
9. She asked her **if she had been busy the week before**.
10. He asked me **which** animal **I was (am)** afraid of.
11. They told us **to listen** to the radio.
12. She asked him **why his** car **had broken down**.

PRESENT PERFECT PROGRESSIVE

The Present Perfect Progressive is used when a long action has started in the past and has just ended (usually recently) or is still continuing. There has to be a connection to the present. The verbs have to express a long period of time.

Key words: all day, how long, for, since

How to form the Present Perfect Progressive

I, you, we, they - **have been + ing form of the verb**
He, she, it - **has been + ing form of the verb**

Short forms

I**'ve** been reading. / They**'ve** been listening.
She**'s** been dancing. / He**'s** been watching.

Negation

I, you, we, they - **have not (haven't) been + ing form of the verb**
He, she, it - **has not (hasn't) been + ing form of the verb**

They haven't been working in the office all day.

Questions

Have they **been helping** you since this morning?
Have/Has - subject - been + ing form of the verb

How long has she **been working** at the office?
Question word - has/have - subject - been + ing form of the verb

Use of the Present Perfect Progressive

Examples:
I **have been working** all day.
She **has been watching** TV since 7.30.
Nick **has been lying** in bed for two days. - He is still in bed or has just got up.
She **has been working** since 4 o'clock. - She is still working, or she has just stopped working.
How long **have** they **been playing**?

PRESENT PERFECT PROGRESSIVE 1

Put the following sentences into the present perfect progressive.

1. It _____ (rain) for hours.
2. Mike _____ (collect) stamps since 1995.
3. Bob _____ (play) tennis since he was seven.
4. I _____ (wait) for the bus for 15 minutes.
5. How long _____ your brother _____ (play) guitar?
6. How long _____ (he play) golf?
7. I _____ (work) for this company for seventeen years.
8. How long _____ (it rain)?
9. Mary _____ (study) German for two years.
10. My grandparents _____ (live) in that house since 1962.
11. My mother _____ (cook) for 3 hours.
12. My sister _____ (drive) since 1972.
13. Peter _____ (live) in India since last month.
14. How long _____ (you work) in the garden?
15. They _____ (lie) in the sun for hours.
16. Why is he so tired? He _____ (play) football for two hours.
17. How long _____ (you work) in the garden?
18. Carol _____ (study) Spanish for four years.
19. Frank and Bill _____ (travel) in Europe for about a month.
20. Samuel _____ (wear) those jeans since Tuesday.
21. How long _____ (you study) English?
22. We _____ (wait) here for three hours.
23. She _____ (watch) too much television lately.
24. I _____ (read) for 3 hours.
25. How long _____ (he wait) for us?

PRESENT PERFECT PROGRESSIVE 2

Put the following sentences into the present perfect simple or progressive.

1. Jane _____ (write) a letter to a magazine. She _____ (not finish) it yet.

2. Ben _____ (look) for his penknife, but he _____ (not find) it yet.

3. Jenny _____ (wait) for the bus for half an hour, but it _____ (not arrive) yet.

4. Nick _____ (play) a computer game for two hours, and he is still playing.

5. Mike _____ (not finished) painting his car yet. He _____ (work) on it for two weeks.

6. Amanda _____ (not come) home yet. She _____ (shop) in town since 10 o'clock.

7. Mike's car _____ (make) strange noises. Nick and Jane _____ (clean) all the parts.

8. Ben _____ (draw) cartoons for two hours. He _____ (not finish) yet.

9. Greg _____ (wait) for Jenny in town. Jenny _____ (not arrive) yet.

10. Jane _____ (knit) a pullover. She _____ (not finish) yet.

11. It _____ (rain) all day, and it _____ (not stop) yet.

12. Mr Blake _____ (make) tests all evening, but he _____ (not find) a perfect one yet.

PRESENT PERFECT PROGRESSIVE 3

Put the following sentences into the present perfect simple or progressive.

1. How often _____ (you clean) the windows this year?

2. I _____ (work) all day and _____ (just come) home from the office.

3. The girls _____ (be) at school since 7 o'clock.

4. I _____ (wait) for the train for half an hour, but it still _____ (not arrive) yet.

5. I _____ (not watch) the new movie yet.

6. She _____ (not cook) anything yet because she _____ (talk) to her neighbour all the time.

7. Amanda _____ (play) seven tournaments this year.

8. It _____ (snow) a lot this week. I hope it will stop soon.

9. Mike _____ (travel) since he finished school.

10. She _____ (work) for the company since she graduated from university.

11. Ben, where have you been? I _____ (wait) for you since 2 o'clock.

12. Many tourists _____ (visit) this museum.

13. It _____ (rain) all week. I hope it will stop by Saturday.

14. She _____ (perform) in eight movies since she began acting.

15. Jane _____ (work) on the computer for hours, and _____ (not finish) yet.

PRESENT PERFECT PROGRESSIVE 4

Put the following sentences into the present perfect simple or progressive.

1. It _____ all day. (rain)
2. How long _____ for me? (you wait)
3. I _____ my girlfriend for two months. (know)
4. I _____ my homework. Now I can go out. (do)
5. I _____ my homework for three hours. (do)
6. What _____ all afternoon? (she do)
   She _____ that book you lent her, but
   she _____ it yet. (read / not finish)
7. Amanda is a famous film star. She _____ about ten films. (make)
8. What countries _____? (you already visit)
9. Mike _____ a cold since last Thursday. (have)
10. I'm tired. _____ very hard today. (work)
11. Susan _____ to reach you by phone several times. (try)
12. He _____ with Kate. (never dance)
13. Someone _____ my chocolate. (eat)
14. How long _____ as a lawyer? (she work)
15. We _____ here for eight years. (live)
16. How long _____ TV this afternoon? (they watch)
17. _____ a mountain? (you ever climb)
18. They _____ the car since three o' clock and they
    _____ yet. (repair / not finish)
19. He _____ at the airport. (already arrive)
20. How long _____ for Linda? (he wait)

PRESENT PERFECT PROGRESSIVE 1

Put the following sentences into the present perfect progressive.

1. It **has been raining** for hours.
2. Mike **has been collecting** stamps since 1995.
3. Bob **has been playing** tennis since he was seven.
4. I **have been waiting** for the bus for 15 minutes.
5. How long **has** your brother **been playing** guitar?
6. How long **has he been playing** golf?
7. I **have been working** for this company for seventeen years.
8. How long **has it been raining**?
9. Mary **has been studying** German for two years.
10. My grandparents **have been living** in that house since 1962.
11. My mother **has been cooking** for 3 hours.
12. My sister **has been driving** since 1972.
13. Peter **has been living** in India since last month.
14. How long **have you been working** in the garden?
15. They **have been lying** in the sun for hours.
16. Why is he so tired? He **has been playing** football for two hours.
17. How long **have you been working** in the garden?
18. Carol **has been studying** Spanish for four years.
19. Frank and Bill **have been travelling** in Europe for about a month.
20. Samuel **has been wearing** those jeans since Tuesday.
21. How long **have you been studying** English?
22. We **have been waiting** here for three hours.
23. She **has been watching** too much television lately.
24. I **have been reading** for 3 hours.
25. How long **has he been waiting** for us?

PRESENT PERFECT PROGRESSIVE 2

Put the following sentences into the present perfect simple or progressive.

1. Jane **has been writing** a letter to a magazine. She **has not finished** it yet.
2. Ben **has been looking** for his penknife, but he **has not found** it yet.
3. Jenny **has been waiting** for the bus for half an hour, but it **has not arrived** yet.
4. Nick **has been playing** a computer game for two hours, and he is still playing.
5. Mike **has not finished** painting his car yet. He **has been working** on it for two weeks.
6. Amanda **has not come** home yet. She **has been shopping** in town since 10 o'clock.
7. Mike's car **has been making** strange noises. Nick and Jane **have cleaned** all the parts.
8. Ben **has been drawing** cartoons for two hours. He **has not finished** yet.
9. Greg **has been waiting** for Jenny in town. Jenny **has not arrived** yet.
10. Jane **has been knitting** a pullover. She **has not finished** yet.
11. It **has been raining** all day, and it **has not stopped** yet.
12. Mr Blake **has been making** tests all evening, but he **has not found** a perfect one yet.

PRESENT PERFECT PROGRESSIVE 3

Put the following sentences into the present perfect simple or progressive.

1. How often **have you cleaned** the windows this year?
2. I **have been working** all day and **have just come** home from the office.
3. The girls **have been** at school since 7 o'clock.
4. I **have been waiting** for the train for half an hour, but it still **hasn't arrived** yet.
5. I **haven't watched** the new movie yet.
6. She **hasn't cooked** anything yet because she **has been talking** to her neighbour all the time.
7. Amanda **has played** seven tournaments this year.
8. It **has been snowing** a lot this week. I hope it will stop soon.
9. Mike **has been travelling** since he finished school.
10. She **has been working** for the company since she graduated from university.
11. Ben, where have you been? I **have been waiting** for you since 2 o'clock.
12. Many tourists **have visited** this museum.
13. It **has been raining** all week. I hope it will stop by Saturday.
14. She **has performed** in eight movies since she began acting.
15. Jane **has been working** on the computer for hours, and she **hasn't finished** yet.

PRESENT PERFECT PROGRESSIVE 4

1. It **has been raining** all day.
2. How long **have you been waiting** for me?
3. I **have known** my girlfriend for two months.
4. I **have done** my homework. Now I can go out.
5. I **have been doing** my homework for three hours.
6. What **has she been doing** all afternoon? She **has been reading** that book you lent her, but she **hasn't finished** it yet.
7. Amanda is a famous film star. She **has made** about ten films.
8. What countries **have you already visited**?
9. Mike **has had** a cold since last Thursday.
10. I'm tired. I **have been working** very hard today.
11. Susan **has tried** to reach you by phone several times.
12. He **has never danced** with Kate.
13. Someone **has eaten** my chocolate.
14. How long **has she been working** as a lawyer?
15. We **have been living** here for eight years.
16. How long **have they been watching** TV this afternoon?
17. **Have you ever climbed** a mountain?
18. They **have been repairing** the car since three o' clock and they **haven't finished** yet.
19. He **has already arrived** at the airport.
20. How long **has he been waiting** for Linda?

PAST PERFECT SIMPLE

If you tell a story it's sometimes necessary to tell about actions that had happened before the past tense. To express the time when these actions happened you have to use the past perfect.

How to form: had (not) + 3rd form

Key words: after, before

Examples:

She needed help because someone **had stolen** her car.
He passed the test because he **had studied** a lot.
After she **had done** her homework, she visited me.
When I came home, they **had** already **eaten**.
They **had sold** everything before they moved to Glasgow.

Forming Questions:

Had she **done** her homework when you visited her?
Had they already **eaten** when you came home?
Had he **sold** everything before he moved?

PAST PERFECT QUESTIONS

Rearrange the words in each sentence to make a question in **past perfect** tense.

1. had the lights off you all switched

   _____ before going to bed?

2. Road lived Jeremy in had Cromer

   _____ for seven years?

3. the their pupils completed had work

   _____ before going out to play?

4. John left already had

   _____ before you got home from work?

5. sold things the had precious she all

   _____ when he came back from his journey?

6. made call had Liam phone a

   _____ by the time his boss appeared?

7. a ever you had career considered

   _____ as a chef before you left school?

8. you to gone just bed had

   _____ when your parents phoned last night?

9. had that seen already you movie

   _____?

10. already the been airport had they at

    _____ before the flight had been cancelled?

PAST PERFECT

Complete the following sentences with the past perfect simple.

1. After they _____ a cup of tea, they had some cake. (have)
2. He told me that he _____ lions the day before. (see)
3. After they _____ lunch, they drank a cup of tea. (finish)
4. Before he went to bed, he _____ to his favourite songs. (listen)
5. My little sister _____ all the jam tarts before her parents came home. (eat)
6. After he _____ the police, he called the ambulance. (call)
7. He told his teacher that he _____ to do his homework. (forget)
8. After they _____ all the famous sights, they went to a restaurant. (see)
9. He asked me which animals I _____ in Africa. (hunt)
10. After Columbus _____ America, he returned to Spain. (discover)
11. Before she typed her letters, she _____ a cup of coffee. (have)
12. After the train _____, they went for a sightseeing tour. (arrive)
13. He _____ to watch TV when the telephone rang. (start)
14. My little brother opened the box after he _____ the key. (get)
15. After he _____ school, he started to work at the butcher's. (finish)
16. When he was young, he _____ a good swimmer. (be)
17. After they _____ for their holidays, their friends arrived. (leave)
18. They _____ everything before they moved to Glasgow. (sell)
19. After she _____ the windows, she washed the curtains. (clean)
20. Before he mowed the lawn, he _____ some roses. (pick)

PAST PERFECT QUESTIONS

1. **Had you switched off all the lights** before going to bed?
2. **Had Jeremy lived in Cromer Road** for seven years?
3. **Had the pupils completed their work** before going out to play?
4. **Had John already left** before you got home from work?
5. **Had she sold all the precious things** when he came back from his journey?
6. **Had Liam made a phone call** by the time his boss appeared?
7. **Had you ever considered a career** as a chef before you left school?
8. **Had you just gone to bed** when your parents phoned last night?
9. **Had you already seen that movie**?
10. **Had they already been at the airport** before the flight had been cancelled?

PAST PERFECT

1. After they **had had** a cup of tea, they had some cake.
2. He told me that he **had seen** lions the day before.
3. After they **had finished** lunch, they drank a cup of tea.
4. Before he went to bed, he **had listened** to his favourite songs.
5. My little sister **had eaten** all the jam tarts before her parents came home.
6. After he **had called** the police, he called the ambulance.
7. He told his teacher that he **had forgotten** to do his homework.
8. After they **had seen** all the famous sights, they went to a restaurant.
9. He asked me which animals I **had hunted** in Africa.
10. After Columbus **had discovered** America, he returned to Spain.
11. Before she typed her letters, she **had had** a cup of coffee.
12. After the train **had arrived**, they went for a sightseeing tour.
13. He **had started** to watch TV when the telephone rang.
14. My little brother opened the box after he **had got / had gotten** the key.
15. After he **had finished** school, he started to work at the butcher's.
16. When he was young, he **had been** a good swimmer.
17. After they **had left** for their holidays, their friends arrived.
18. They **had sold** everything before they moved to Glasgow.
19. After she **had cleaned** the windows, she washed the curtains.
20. Before he mowed the lawn, he **had picked** some roses.

PAST TENSE OR PAST PERFECT 1

Complete the following sentences with the past simple, past progressive or past perfect simple.

1. After they _____ a cup of tea, they _____ some cake. (have / have)

2. They _____ the flat two years ago. (buy)

3. When I _____ TV, the lights _____ (watch / go out)

4. She _____ me that she _____ a lion. (tell / see)

5. He _____ to France last year. (go)

6. After he _____ the ambulance, he _____ the police. (call / call)

7. She _____ her hair when her baby _____ to cry. (wash / start)

8. After he _____ hard, he _____ ill. (work / feel)

9. He _____ the room when I _____ the facts. (leave / explain)

10. Dad _____ the box after he _____ the key. (open / find)

11. While he _____ computer games, she _____ (play / read)

12. They _____ everything before they _____ to Glasgow. (sell / move)

13. My sister _____ me yesterday evening. (visit)

14. When I _____ the room, Mary _____ home. (clean / come)

15. After he _____ school, he _____ to work. (finish / start)

PAST TENSE OR PAST PERFECT 2

Complete the following sentences with the past simple, past progressive or past perfect simple.

1. When they _____ (sleep), thieves _____ (break) in and _____ (steal) their paintings.
2. After he _____ (repair) his bike, he _____ (drive) to his grandparents.
3. Before she _____ (have) dinner, she _____ (work) in the garden.
4. I _____ (see) him yesterday in front of the cinema.
5. When they _____ (listen) to music, they _____ (hear) a loud noise.
6. He _____ (not visit) me before he _____ (fly) to Greece.
7. My sister _____ (hear) a loud cry from outside and _____ (rush) out.
8. While she _____ (study) for her test, her brother _____ (play) football with his friends.
9. We _____ (not play) chess last Sunday.
10. He _____ (go) shopping after he _____ (phone) me.
11. When we _____ (meet) Jane at the party, she _____ (wear) a red dress.
12. She _____ (not drive) fast when the accident _____ (happen).
13. The boys _____ (break) a window when they _____ (play) football in the garden.
14. Mary _____ (not work) yesterday. She _____ (be) ill.
15. After she _____ (help) me with the housework, she _____ (go) to meet her friends.

PAST TENSE OR PAST PERFECT 1

1. After they **had had** a cup of tea, they **had** some cake.
2. They **bought** the flat two years ago.
3. When I **was watching** TV, the lights **went out**.
4. She **told** me that she **had seen** a lion.
5. He **went** to France last year.
6. After he **had called** the ambulance, he **called** the police.
7. She **was washing** her hair when her baby **started** to cry.
8. After he **had worked** hard, he **felt** ill.
9. He **left** the room when I **had explained** the facts.
10. Dad **opened** the box after he **had found** the key.
11. While he **was playing** computer games, she **was reading.**
12. They **had sold** everything before they **moved** to Glasgow.
13. My sister **visited** me yesterday evening.
14. When I **was cleaning** the room, Mary **came** home.
15. After he **had finished** school, he **started** to work.

PAST TENSE OR PAST PERFECT 2

1. When they **were sleeping**, thieves **broke** in and **stole** their paintings.
2. After he **had repaired** his bike, he **drove** to his grandparents.
3. Before she **had** dinner, she **had worked** in the garden.
4. I **saw** him yesterday in front of the cinema.
5. When they **were listening** to music, they **heard** a loud noise.
6. He **had not visited** me before he **flew** to Greece.
7. My sister **heard** a loud cry from outside and **rushed** out.
8. While she **was studying** for her test, her brother **was playing** football with his friends.
9. We **did not play** chess last Sunday.
10. He **went** shopping after he **had phoned** me.
11. When we **met** Jane at the party, she **was wearing** a red dress.
12. She **was not driving** fast when the accident **happened**.
13. The boys **broke** a window when they **were playing** football in the garden.
14. Mary **did not work** yesterday. She **was** ill.
15. After she **had helped** me with the housework, she **went** to meet her friends.

PAST SIMPLE OR PAST PERFECT 1

Complete the following sentences with the past simple or past perfect simple.

1. After they _____ (see) the Tower, they _____ (go) to Westminster Abbey.
2. He _____ (ask) me which animals I _____ (see) in Africa.
3. After Columbus _____ (discover) America, he _____ (return) to Spain.
4. Before they _____ (move) to Liverpool, they _____ (sell) everything.
5. After he _____ (work) very hard, he _____ (fall) ill.
6. She _____ (open) the box after she _____ (find) the key.
7. They _____ (go) to a restaurant after they _____ (sail).
8. Before they _____ (start) the party, they _____ (invite) some friends.
9. After she _____ (wash) the curtains, she _____ (clean) the windows.
10. They _____ (go) for a sightseeing tour after the bus _____ (arrive).
11. Before he _____ (mow) the lawn, he _____ (pick) some roses.
12. After he _____ (finish) school, he _____ (work) for a magazine.
13. They _____ (drink) a cup of tea after they _____ (finish) lunch.
14. My friend _____ (ask) me for her telephone number before he _____ (phone) her.
15. My sister _____ (eat) all the chocolate before my parents _____ (come) home.

PAST SIMPLE OR PAST PERFECT 2

Complete the following sentences with the past simple or past perfect simple.

1. After they _____ (open) the window, it _____ (become) colder.
2. After we _____ (see) the film, we _____ (go) to bed.
3. After he _____ (leave), she _____ (start) to cry.
4. As soon as it _____ (start) to rain, she _____ (take) her umbrella.
5. He _____ (play) cards after he _____ (do) his homework.
6. Before she _____ (thank) me, she _____ (take) my present.
7. We _____ (see) the robbers after they _____ (leave) the bank.
8. She _____ (comb) his hair after she _____ (brush) her teeth.
9. Before we _____ (go) out, we _____ (put) on our new shoes.
10. They _____ (go) swimming after it _____ (stop) raining.
11. When we _____ (arrive) there, the ceremony _____ (already start).
12. Father _____ (start) to wash the car after mother _____ (go) out.
13. After she _____ (got) her new dress, she _____ (show) it her parents.
14. He _____ (fall) from the balcony after he _____ (take) away the railing.
15. She _____ (eat) the cake after she _____ (ask).

PAST SIMPLE OR PAST PERFECT 3

Complete the following sentences with the past simple or past perfect simple.

1. He _____ (work) in a supermarket before he _____ (work) as a postman.
2. She _____ (feed) the dog as soon as she _____ (do) her homework.
3. My sister _____ (live) in England before she _____ (move) to Belgium.
4. After he _____ (eat) all the sandwiches, he _____ (drink) some orange juice.
5. We _____ (be) tired because we _____ (work) all day.
6. As I _____ (miss) the bus, I _____ (walk) home again.
7. After they _____ (install) the file, they _____ (can) go on working.
8. He _____ (just start) to watch TV when the telephone _____ (ring).
9. Before she _____ (go) to bed, she _____ (listen) to music.
10. After he _____ (lose) all his money, he _____ (be) as poor as a church mouse.
11. She _____ (have) a cup of coffee before she _____ (write) the letter.
12. My sister _____ (eat) all the jam before our parents _____ (come) home.
13. Tom _____ (be) very angry because Ann _____ (shout) at him.
14. She _____ (go) home again as soon as she _____ (do) her shopping.
15. They _____ (go) to a sightseeing tour after the bus _____ (arrive).

PAST SIMPLE OR PAST PERFECT 4

Complete the following sentences with the past simple or past perfect simple.

1. John _____ (play) with the children after he _____ (have) dinner.
2. The farmer _____ (harvest) the apples before he _____ (take) them to his neighbour to make cider.
3. After it _____ (stop) raining, the match _____ (can) start.
4. After George _____ (swallow) his medicine, he _____ (begin) to feel much better.
5. Before he _____ (become) president, he _____ (work) as an actor.
6. The tourists _____ (jump) into the pool as soon as they _____ (unpack) their suitcases.
7. They _____ (sell) their flat, before they _____ (move) to the Netherlands.
8. He _____ (work) as a tourist agent after he _____ (finish) school.
9. After he _____ (call) the police, he _____ (call) the ambulance.
10. We _____ (leave) the cinema as soon as the movie _____ (end).
11. After Mary _____ (get) her new school uniform, she _____ (be) very happy.
12. He _____ (meet) some friends after he _____ (study) for the test.
13. When we _____ (arrive) at home, she _____ (already do) the washing.
14. She _____ (need) help because someone _____ (steal) her money.
15. She _____ (do) her homework before she _____ (visit) me.

PAST SIMPLE OR PAST PERFECT 1

1. After they **had seen** (see) the Tower, they **went** (go) to Westminster Abbey.
2. He **asked** (ask) me which animals I **had seen** (see) in Africa.
3. After Columbus **had discovered** (discover) America, he **returned** (return) to Spain.
4. Before they **moved** (move) to Liverpool, they **had sold** (sell) everything.
5. After he **had worked** (work) very hard, he **fell** (fall) ill.
6. She **opened** (open) the box after she **had found** (find) the key.
7. They **went** (go) to a restaurant after they **had sailed** (sail).
8. Before they **started** (start) the party, they **had invited** (invite) some friends.
9. After she **had washed** (wash) the curtains, she **cleaned** (clean) the windows.
10. They **went** (go) for a sightseeing tour after the bus **had arrived** (arrive).
11. Before he **mowed** (mow) the lawn, he **had picked** (pick) some roses.
12. After he **had finished** (finish) school, he **worked** (work) for a magazine.
13. They **drank** (drink) a cup of tea after they **had finished** (finish) lunch.
14. My friend **had asked** (ask) me for her telephone number before he **phoned** (phone) her.
15. My sister **had eaten** (eat) all the chocolate before my parents **came** (come) home.

PAST SIMPLE OR PAST PERFECT 2

1. After they **had opened** (open) the window, it **became** (become) colder.
2. After we **had seen** (see) the film, we **went** (go) to bed.
3. After he **had left** (leave), she **started** (start) to cry.
4. As soon as it **had started** (start) to rain, she **took** (take) her umbrella.
5. He **played** (play) cards after he **had done** (do) his homework.
6. Before she **thanked** (thank) me, she **had taken** (take) my present.
7. We **saw** (see) the robbers after they **had left** (leave) the bank.
8. She **combed** (comb) his hair after she **had brushed** (brush) her teeth.
9. Before we **went** (go) out, we **had put** (put) on our new shoes.
10. They **went** (go) swimming after it **had stopped** (stop) raining.
11. When we **arrived** (arrive) there, the ceremony **had already started** (already start).
12. Father **started** (start) to wash the car after mother **had gone** (go) out.
13. After she **had got** (got) her new dress, she **showed** (show) it her parents.
14. He **fell** (fall) from the balcony after he **had taken** (take) away the railing.
15. She **ate** (eat) the cake after she **had asked** (ask).

PAST SIMPLE OR PAST PERFECT 3

1. He **had worked** (work) in a supermarket before he **worked** (work) as a postman.
2. She **fed** (feed) the dog as soon as she **had done** (do) her homework.
3. My sister **had lived** (live) in England before she **moved** (move) to Belgium.
4. After he **had eaten** (eat) all the sandwiches, he **drank** (drink) some orange juice.
5. We **were** (be) tired because we **had worked** (work) all day.
6. As I **had missed** (miss) the bus, I **walked** (walk) home again.
7. After they **had installed** (install) the file, they **could** (can) go on working.
8. He **had just started** (just start) to watch TV when the telephone **rang** (ring).
9. Before she **went** (go) to bed, she **had listened** (listen) to her favourite CD.
10. After he **had lost** (lose) all his money, he **was** (be) as poor as a church mouse.
11. She **had had** (have) a cup of coffee before she **wrote** (write) the letter.
12. My sister **had eaten** (eat) all the jam before our parents **came** (come) home.
13. Tom **was** (be) very angry because Ann **had shouted** (shout) at him.
14. She **went** (go) home again as soon as she **had done** (do) her shopping.
15. They **went** (go) to a sightseeing tour after the bus **had arrived** (arrive).

PAST SIMPLE OR PAST PERFECT 4

1. John **played** (play) with the children after he **had had** (have) dinner.
2. The farmer **had harvested** (harvest) the apples before he **took** (take) them to his neighbour to make cider.
3. After it **had stopped** (stop) raining, the tennis match **could** (can) start.
4. After George **had swallowed** (swallow) his medicine, he **began** (begin) to feel much better.
5. Before he **became** (become) president, he **had worked** (work) as an actor.
6. The tourists **jumped** (jump) into the pool as soon as they **had unpacked** (unpack) their suitcases.
7. They **had sold** (sell) their flat, before they **moved** (move) to the Netherlands.
8. He **worked** (work) as a tourist agent after he **had finished** (finish) school.
9. After he **had called** (call) the police, he **called** (call) the ambulance.
10. We **left** (leave) the cinema as soon as the movie **had ended** (end).
11. After Mary **had got** (get) her new school uniform, she **was** (be) very happy.
12. He **met** (meet) some friends after he **had studied** (study) for the test.
13. When we **arrived** (arrive) at home, she **had already done** (already do) the washing.
14. She **needed** (need) help because someone **had stolen** (steal) her money.
15. She **had done** (do) her homework before she **visited** (visit) me.

TENSES

PRESENT SIMPLE

1st form / he, she, it **+ s** // they go, he goes

It's used with habits and general statements
Key words: **always, often, usually, every, never, generally, seldom, rarely, hardly ever, sometimes, normally**

PAST SIMPLE

2nd form // he went, they played

It's used to tell or talk about a past action.
Key words: **yesterday, last, ago, in 1970**

WILL FUTURE

will + 1st form (N.: won't) // he will be, she will go

It's used to talk about the future.
Key words: **tomorrow, next**

PRESENT PERFECT SIMPLE

have / has + 3rd form // she has gone

It's used when a past action started in the past and has just finished or is still happening.
Key words: **already, just, ever, never, yet, for, since**

PAST PERFECT SIMPLE

had + 3rd form // she had gone

It's used when an action happened before another action.
Key words: **after, before**

PRESENT PROGRESSIVE

am / is / are + verb + ing // I am going

It's used when something is happening at the moment.
Key words: **look, listen, now, at the moment**

PAST PROGRESSIVE

was / were + ing form // he was going

It's used to tell or talk about a long action in the past.
Key words: **while, when**

GOING TO FUTURE

am / is / are + going to + verb
He is going to play tennis tomorrow.

It's used to talk about a future action that is planned.
Key words: **tomorrow, next**

PRESENT PERFECT PROGRESSIVE

have / has + been + ing form // he has been going

It's used like the simple form, but only with long actions.

Key words: **how long, all day, for, since**

PAST PERFECT PROGRESSIVE

had been + ing form // he had been going

It's used like the simple form, but only with long actions.

Key words: **how long, before, after**

TENSES 1

Write down the sentences. Use the correct forms of the verbs.
N = negation / Q = question

They (invite) Linda to the party.
Present tense: _____

    N: _____

    Q: _____

Past tense: _____

    N: _____

    Q: _____

Future: _____

    N: _____

    Q: _____

Present perfect: _____

    N: _____

    Q: _____

They (be) happy.
Present tense: _____

    N: _____

    Q: _____

Past tense: _____

    N: _____

    Q: _____

Future: _____

    N: _____

    Q: _____

Present perfect: _____

    N: _____

    Q: _____

TENSES 2

Write down the sentences. Use the correct forms of the verbs.
N = negation / Q = question

He (leave) in the afternoon.
Present tense: _____

                N: _____

                Q: _____

Past tense: _____

                N: _____

                Q: _____

Future: _____

                N: _____

                Q: _____

Present perfect: _____

                N: _____

                Q: _____

The children (play) tennis.
Present tense: _____

                N: _____

                Q: _____

Past tense: _____

                N: _____

                Q: _____

Future: _____

                N: _____

                Q: _____

Present perfect: _____

                N: _____

                Q: _____

TENSES 1

Present tense: They **invite** Linda to the party.
    N: They **don't** (do not) **invite** Linda to the party.
    Q: **Do they invite** Linda to the party?

Past tense: They **invited** Linda to the party.
    N: They **didn't** (did not) **invite** Linda to the party.
    Q: **Did they invite** Linda to the party?

Future: They **will invite** Linda to the party.
    N: They **will not** (won't) **invite** Linda to the party
    Q: **Will they invite** Linda to the party?

Present perfect: They **have invited** Linda to the party.
    N: They **haven't** (have not) **invited** Linda to the party.
    Q: **Have they invited** Linda to the party?

Present tense: They **are** happy.
    N: They **aren't** (are not) happy.
    Q: **Are they** happy?

Past tense: They **were** happy.
    N: They **weren't** (were not) happy.
    Q: **Were they** happy?

Future: They **will be** happy.
    N: They **will not** (won't) **be** happy.
    Q: **Will they be** happy?

Present perfect: They **have been** happy.
    N: They **haven't** (have not) **been** happy.
    Q: **Have they been** happy?

TENSES 2

Present tense:　　He **leaves** in the afternoon.
　　　　　　　　N: He **doesn't** (does not) **leave** in the afternoon.
　　　　　　　　Q: **Does he leave** in the afternoon?
Past tense:　　　He **left** in the afternoon.
　　　　　　　　N: He **didn't** (did not) **leave** in the afternoon.
　　　　　　　　Q: **Did he leave** in the afternoon?
Future:　　　　　He **will leave** in the afternoon.
　　　　　　　　N: He **will not** (won't) **leave** in the afternoon.
　　　　　　　　Q: **Will he leave** in the afternoon?
Present perfect:　He **has left** in the afternoon.
　　　　　　　　N: He **hasn't** (has not) **left** in the afternoon.
　　　　　　　　Q: **Has he left** in the afternoon?

Present tense:　　The children **play** tennis.
　　　　　　　　N: The children **don't** (do not) **play** tennis.
　　　　　　　　Q: **Do the children play** tennis?
Past tense:　　　The children **played** tennis.
　　　　　　　　N: The children **didn't** (did not) **play** tennis.
　　　　　　　　Q: **Did the children play** tennis?
Future:　　　　　The children **will play** tennis.
　　　　　　　　N: The children **will not** (won't) **play** tennis.
　　　　　　　　Q: **Will** the children **play** tennis?
Present perfect:　The children **have played** tennis.
　　　　　　　　N: The children **haven't** (have not) **played** tennis.
　　　　　　　　Q: **Have** the children **played** tennis?

MIXED TENSES 1

Fill in the correct tenses.

1. Look! It _____ (snow) now.
2. She _____ (have) the flue last winter.
3. Last night I _____ (read) a book when suddenly I _____ (hear) a scream.
4. Carol _____ (already start) her new job.
5. Last week my rabbit _____ (run) away, and I _____ (find) it yet.
6. The teacher _____ (write) sentences on the board while the children _____ (fill) the gaps.
7. Water _____ (boil) at 100 degrees Celsius.
8. What _____ Peter _____ (do) at the moment? He _____ (have) a bath.
9. I _____ (go) to the theatre yesterday evening.
10. _____ you ever _____ (write) a letter to Sue? Yes, I _____ (write) her yesterday.
11. When I _____ (wait) for the bus, I _____ (see) an accident.
12. George often _____ (work) on Sundays.
13. _____ you _____ (do) your homework yet?
14. He _____ (have) a bad accident last evening.
15. Sandra _____ (get) a bad mark on her last maths test.
16. Tom _____ (repair) the car now.
17. Excuse me, _____ you _____ (speak) English?
18. Where _____ (be) Peggy? She _____ (leave) an hour ago.
19. I _____ (be) very nervous last Saturday because I _____ never _____ (fly) before.
20. How often _____ you _____ (play) tennis? I usually _____ (play) once a week.

MIXED TENSES 2

Fill in the correct tenses.

1. _____ John ever _____ (win) a prize at a race?
2. I _____ (fall) asleep yesterday when I _____ (watch) TV.
3. George _____ never _____ (be) to Canada.
4. Tom is back in England. He _____ (be) in Italy for three weeks.
5. We _____ (do) a lot last Sunday.
6. I sometimes _____ (go) to the cinema.
7. Nick _____ (work) hard yesterday.
8. I _____ (find) my ring yet which I _____ (lose) at the party yesterday.
9. They _____ (build) this castle in 1762.
10. Would you like to have something to eat? No, thank you I _____ (just have) dinner.
11. Sue _____ (get) up at 6 o´clock every day.
12. Look! Sue _____ (run) down the street.
13. This house _____ (cost) 35.000 pounds in 1980.
14. Cats _____ (catch) mice.
15. _____ you _____ (meet) Bill yesterday?
16. When he _____ (arrive), we _____ (have) dinner.
17. _____ he _____ (already arrive) in Los Angeles?
18. I _____ (see) him since last Wednesday.
19. Father _____ (smoke) his pipe while mother _____ (prepare) lunch.
20. Look, it _____ (snow)

MIXED TENSES 3

Fill in the correct tenses.

1. I usually _____ (take) the bus to school.
2. Yesterday morning I _____ (get) up at 6.30.
3. We needed some money so we _____ (sell) our car.
4. He asked me, "_____ she ever _____ (be) in Spain?"
5. My mother asked us, "What _____ Peter _____ (do) now?"
6. Please don´t make so much noise. I _____ (study).
7. We can leave. Samantha _____ her car keys. (just find)
8. Carol often _____ (play) tennis with her father.
9. Now Ron _____ (phone) Jill again. It _____ (be) the third time he _____ (phone) her this evening.
10. It _____ (rain) now. It _____ (begin) raining two hours ago. So, it _____ (rain) for two hours.
11. She asked me, "_____ you _____ (hear) from Tom?"
12. "_____ it _____ (rain)?" she always _____ (ask) me.
13. I asked my brother, "_____ you _____ (go) out last night?"
14. New York _____ (be) one of the largest cities of the world.
15. This house _____ (cost) 350.000 pounds in 1980.
16. While Tom _____ (play) tennis, Ann _____ (take) a shower.
17. Mike _____ (play) chess. How long _____ (play)?
18. "_____ you _____ (speak) English?" she was asked.
19. When they _____ (work) in the garden, the phone _____ (ring).
20. After they _____ (have) their breakfast, they _____ (go) shopping yesterday.

MIXED TENSES 4

Fill in the correct tenses.

1. She often _____ trouble with her parents. (have)

2. Richard _____ two bottles of orange juice last night. (drink)

3. Last week they _____ a new car and _____ the old one. (buy / sell)

4. After he _____ TV, he went to bed yesterday. (watch)

5. Little Toby _____ his hands. They are clean now. (just wash)

6. Last evening when he _____ a book his mother _____ him. (read / call)

7. I think we _____ to Spain for our holidays next summer. (go)

8. We always _____ her to wash her hands, but she never _____ it. (tell / do)

9. This _____ the most exciting film I _____! (be / ever see)

10. If I _____ you, I would try to marry this pretty girl. (be)

11. In spring birds _____ and in summer they _____ nests. (sing / build)

12. Every year the number of students who come to Britain _____. (increase)

13. If you _____ us, we would have met you at the station. (call)

14. Every morning old Mr. Sharp _____ from a small boat. (fish)

15. Last Saturday when we went to the Millers, they _____ cards. (play)

16. Look at this picture. This _____ the Prime Minister's home. (be)

17. Yesterday we _____ anything because of the thick fog. (cannot see)

18. We can leave. Samantha _____ her car keys. (just find)

MIXED TENSES 1

1. Look! It **is snowing** now.
2. She **had** the flue last winter.
3. Last night I **was reading** a book when suddenly I **heard** a scream.
4. Carol **has already started** her new job.
5. Last week my rabbit **ran** away, and I **haven't found** it yet.
6. The teacher **was writing** sentences on the board while the children **were filling** the gaps.
7. Water **boils** at 100 degrees Celsius.
8. What **is** Peter **doing** at the moment? He **is having** a bath.
9. I **went** to the theatre yesterday evening.
10. **Have** you ever **written** a letter to Sue? Yes, I **wrote** her yesterday.
11. When I **was waiting** for the bus, I **saw** an accident.
12. George often **works** on Sundays.
13. **Have** you **done** your homework yet?
14. He **had** a bad accident last evening.
15. Sandra **got** a bad mark on her last maths test.
16. Tom **is repairing** the car now.
17. Excuse me, **do** you **speak** English?
18. Where **is** Peggy? She **left** an hour ago.
19. I **was** very nervous last Saturday because I **have** never **flown** before.
20. How often **do** you **play** tennis? I usually **play** once a week.

MIXED TENSES 2

1. **Has** John ever **won** a prize at a race?
2. I **fell** asleep yesterday when I **was watching** TV.
3. George **has** never **been** to Canada.
4. Tom is back in England. He **has been** in Italy for three weeks.
5. We **did** a lot last Sunday.
6. I sometimes **go** to the cinema.
7. Nick **worked** hard yesterday.
8. I **haven't found** my ring yet which I **lost** at the party yesterday.
9. They **built** this castle in 1762.
10. Would you like to have something to eat? No, thank you I **have just had** dinner.
11. Sue **gets** up at 6 o'clock every day.
12. Look! Sue **is running** down the street.
13. This house **cost** 35.000 pounds in 1980.
14. Cats **catch** mice.
15. **Did** you **meet** Bill yesterday?
16. When he **arrived,** we **were having** dinner.
17. **Has** he **already arrived** in Los Angeles?
18. I **haven't seen** him since last Wednesday.
19. Father **is smoking** his pipe while mother **was preparing** lunch.
20. Look, it **is snowing**.

MIXED TENSES 3

1. I usually **take** the bus to school.
2. Yesterday morning I **got up** at 6.30.
3. We needed some money, so we **sold** our car.
4. He asked me, "**Has** she ever **been** in Spain? "
5. My mother asked us, "What **is** Peter **doing** now?"
6. Please don´t make so much noise. I **am studying**.
7. We can leave. Samantha **has just found** her car keys.
8. Carol often **plays** tennis with her father.
9. Now Ron **is phoning** Jill again. It **is** (be) the third time he **has phoned** her this evening.
10. It **is raining** now. It **has begun** raining two hours ago. So, it **has been raining** for two hours.
11. She asked me, "**Have** you **heard** from Tom?"
12. "**Is** it **raining**?" she always **asks** me.
13. I asked my brother, "**Did** you **go** out last night?"
14. New York **is** one of the largest cities of the world.
15. This house **cost** 350.000 pounds in 1980.
16. While Tom **was playing** tennis, Ann **was taking** a shower.
17. Mike **is playing** chess. How long **has he been playing**?
18. **Do** you **speak** English?" she was asked.
19. When they **were working** (work) in the garden, the phone **rang**.
20. After they **had had** their breakfast, they **went** shopping yesterday.

MIXED TENSES 4

1. She often **has** trouble with her parents.
2. Richard **drank** two bottles of orange juice last night.
3. Last week they **bought** a new car and **sold** the old one.
4. After he **had watched** TV, he went to bed yesterday.
5. Little Toby **has just washed** his hands. They are clean now.
6. Last evening when he **was reading** a book his mother **called** him.
7. I think we **will go** to Spain for our holidays next summer.
8. We always **tell** her to wash her hands, but she never **does** it.
9. This **is** the most exciting film I **have ever seen**!
10. If I **was/were** you, I would try to marry this pretty girl.
11. In spring birds **sing** and in summer they **build** nests.
12. Every year the number of students who come to Britain **increases**.
13. If you **had called** us, we would have met you at the station.
14. Every morning old Mr. Sharp **fishes** from a small boat.
15. Last Saturday when we went to the Millers, they **were playing** cards.
16. Look at this picture. This **is** the Prime Minister's home.
17. Yesterday we **couldn't see** anything because of the thick fog.
18. We can leave. Samantha **has just found** her car keys.

WORD ORDER

Adverb of place, time	Subject	Adverb of indefinite time	Verb	Object	Adverb of manner	Adverb of place	Adverb of time
Yesterday	Nick		bought	a pair of skis		in Innsbruck.	
In Innsbruck	Nick		bought	a pair of skis			yesterday.
	He		bought	a pair of skis			
	He		practiced		hard	on a ski slope	yesterday.
In the morning	he	always	has	lessons		on a ski slope	
After dinner	he	usually	meets	a friend		at the bar	

NOTE: If there are two adverbs of time the precise one is first!
Example: He is going to have a skiing lesson **at 10 a.m.** on Monday.

NOTE: A verb is sometimes **two or more words**! Then the adverb of indefinite time has to be put between them:

	verb 1	adverb	verb 2	
I	can	**never**	remember	his name.
Ann	doesn't	**usually**	smoke	
	Are you	**definitely**	going	to the party?
Your car	has	**probably**	been stolen	
He	has	**never**	tried skiing	

NOTE: Adverbs of indefinite time go **before have to**!
Example: We **always** have to wait a long time for the bus.

NOTE: Adverbs of indefinite time go **after am, is, are, was or were**!
Example: You are **never** on time.

WORD ORDER 1

Write down the sentences into correct order.

1. always / at nine o'clock / out of the garage / in the morning / drives / his car / he

2. he / to town / after breakfast / often / Mrs Hodges / takes

3. a parking place / near the shops / they / find / rarely

4. sometimes / in a garage / Mr Hodges / his car / parks

5. fly / with my parents / to Florida / sometimes / I / in winter

6. late / came / last year / she / often / to school / in spring

7. often / have / at about three o'clock / a cup of tea / they / at the hotel / in the afternoon

8. meet / at the sports ground / they / after dinner / always / their friends

9. enjoys / very much / swimming / in our pool / always / in the morning / she

10. hardly / last year / could / ski / he

WORD ORDER 2

Write down the sentences into correct order.

1. hardly / the / feeds / My / ever / dog / brother

   _____

2. sister / ironing / sometimes / My / the / does

   _____

3. I / vacuum / never / the / do / cleaning

   _____

4. a / go / with / often / walk / dog / for / We / our

   _____

5. room / Sundays / usually / I / tidy / my / on

   _____

6. the / unload / in / the / sometimes / afternoon / dishwasher / I

   _____

7. after / on / my / I / sister / look / weekends / sometimes / younger

   _____

8. never / the / She / cooking / does

   _____

9. mother / On / the / my / always / washing / does / Mondays

   _____

10. out / once / put / I / dustbins / week / usually / the / a

    _____

WORD ORDER 3

Write down the sentences into correct order.

1. is / near / school / there / new / a / our / cinema

2. got / my / problem / I / with / have / homework / a

3. when / a / helps / she / thinks / problem / trouble / Mary / has / doll / her / a

4. well / think / your / very / I / don't / father / drives

5. to / we / On / a / restaurant / sometimes / Sundays / go

6. circus / went / with / we / ago, / the / two / my / to / parents / months

7. did / very / the / trick / well / magician / his

8. after / Jim / sister / Mother / look / asked / his / to / younger

9. her / Cindy / you / I / found / can / tell / that / have / necklace

10. way / on / bike / Mike / on / already / been / his / to / his / school / has

WORD ORDER 4

Write down the sentences into correct order.

1. o'clock / by / are / sure / make / you / eight / here

2. Ireland / liked / much / in / was / month / very / I / and / last / there / it / I

3. arrested / murder / man / the / who / a / of / was / police / guilty

4. George / bus / morning / work / the / every / to / takes

5. news, / phoned / immediately / When / I / heard / her / the / I

6. shopping / Monday / open / mall / next / will / the / new

7. minutes / name / remembered / after / her / few / I / a

8. tried / before / you / this / Have / ever

9. days / going / for / Boston / week / to / I'm / few / next / a

10. see / party / you / Tom's / Friday / didn't / at / last / I

11. alarm / immediately / got / rang, / the / of / the / When / bed / out / I

12. were / while / couldn't / find / for / We / for / but / looking / a / it / it

WORD ORDER 5

Write down the sentences into correct order.

1. party / met / This / girl / Friday / the / last / at / is / I / Nora's

   _____

2. usually / golf / morning / every / play / They / Sunday

   _____

3. are / new / end / shopping / at / centre / my / the / a / street / building / They / of

   _____

4. the / moment / breakfast / Is / making / the / she / at

   _____

5. about / o'clock / morning / arrived / ten / He / the / at / in

   _____

6. probably / this / home / arrive / late / evening / I'll / at

   _____

7. won't / come / be / afraid / to / meeting / I'm / the / I / to / able

   _____

8. work / don't / I / on / have / Saturdays / to

   _____

9. much / than / will / weather / The / better / today / be / tomorrow

   _____

10. Madrid / were / down / their / their / on / They / when / broke / way / car / to

    _____

11. sometimes / at / school / visit / me / My / after / work / daughters

    _____

12. morning / always / have / too / because / hurry / the / to / get / late / in / I / up / I

    _____

WORD ORDER 1

1. He always drives his car out of the garage at nine o'clock in the morning.
2. He often takes Mrs Hodges to town after breakfast.
3. They rarely find a parking place near the shops.
4. Mr Hodges sometimes parks his car in a garage.
5. I sometimes fly with my parents to Florida in winter.
6. She often came late to school in spring last year.
7. They often have a cup of tea at the hotel at about three o'clock in the afternoon.
8. They always meet their friends at the sports ground after dinner.
9. She always enjoys swimming very much in our pool in the morning.
10. He could hardly ski last year.

WORD ORDER 2

1. My brother hardly ever feeds the dog.
2. My sister sometimes does the ironing.
3. I never do the vacuum cleaning.
4. We often go for a walk with our dog.
5. I usually tidy my room on Sundays.
6. In the afternoon I sometimes unload the dishwasher.
   I sometimes unload the dishwasher in the afternoon.
7. I sometimes look after my younger sister on weekends.
8. She never does the cooking.
9. On Mondays my mother always does the washing.
10. I usually put out the dustbins once a week.

WORD ORDER 3

1. There is a new cinema near our school.
2. I have got a problem with my homework.
3. Mary thinks a trouble doll helps her when she has a problem.
4. I don't think your father drives very well.
5. On Sundays we sometimes go to a restaurant.
6. Two months ago, we went to the circus with my parents.
7. The magician did his trick very well.
8. Mother asked Jim to look after his younger sister.
9. Can you tell Cindy that I have found her necklace?
10. Mike has already been on his way to school on his bike.

WORD ORDER 4

1. Make sure you are here by eight o'clock.
2. I was in Ireland last month and I liked it very much there.
3. The police arrested a man who was guilty of murder.
4. Every morning George takes the bus to work.
5. When I heard the news, I phoned her immediately.
6. The new shopping mall will open next Monday.
7. I remembered her name after a few minutes.
8. Have you ever tried this before?
9. I'm going to Boston for a few days next week.
10. I didn't see you at Tom's party last Friday.
11. When the alarm rang, I got out of the bed immediately.
12. We were looking for it for a while but couldn't find it.

WORD ORDER 5

1. This is the girl I met at Nora's party last Friday.
2. They usually play golf every Sunday morning.
3. They are building a new shopping centre at the end of my street.
4. Is she making the breakfast at the moment?
5. He arrived at about ten o'clock in the morning.
6. I'll probably arrive at home late this evening.
7. I'm afraid I won't be able to come to the meeting.
8. I don't have to work on Saturdays.
9. The weather will be much better tomorrow than today.
10. They were on their way to Madrid when their car broke down.
11. My daughters sometimes visit me at work after school.
12. I always have to hurry in the morning because I get up too late. Or I have to hurry in the morning because I always get up too late.

GERUND OR INFINITIVE

There are verbs which are followed by a gerund and verbs which are followed by an infinitive. Study the following lists and study them before doing the exercises.

These verbs are followed by a gerund (ing noun):
admit, advise, allow, anticipate, appreciate, avoid, can't help, carry on, complete, consider, defend, delay, deny, despise, detest, discuss, dislike, enjoy, fancy, feel, like, finish, give up, imagine, insist on, involve, justify, keep (on), mention, mind, miss, not mind, postpone, practise, put off, recall, recollect, recommend, reject, report, resent, resist, risk, save, suggest, tolerate, understand

These verbs are followed by to + infinitive:
afford, agree, aim, appear, arrange, ask, attempt, care, choose, claim, dare, decide, demand, deserve, expect, fail, happen, help, hesitate, hope, intend, learn, long, manage, need, offer, plan, prepare, pretend, proceed, promise, refuse, seem, swear, tend, threaten, try, turn out, vow, wait, want, wish, would like

These verbs can be followed by either a gerund or to + infinitive:
begin, bother, can't bear, can't stand, cease, continue, forget*, go on*, hate, intend, like, love, mean*, prefer, propose, regret*, remember*, start, stop*, try

*These verbs change their meaning depending on the form that follows them.
If these verbs are followed by a gerund, the gerund refers to an action which that happened before the main verb.
If these verbs are followed by an infinitive, the infinitive refers to an action that happened at the same time or after the main verb.

GERUND OR INFINITIVE 1

Fill in either a gerund or an infinitive.

1. After two weeks of discussion we have agreed _____ you the job. (give)

2. You would do well to avoid _____ the motorway this morning. (take)

3. There would be an outcry if we publicly discussed _____ the National Health Service. (privatise)

4. It was tough, but Polly finally admitted _____ the jewellery. (steal)

5. If Harold had disliked _____ the apple pie, I wouldn't have offered him any more. (eat)

6. My daughter sometimes asks me _____ her with her homework. (help)

7. I think you will really enjoy _____ my parents on Friday. (meet)

8. It can't have been easy for Barry to give up _____. (smoke)

9. I hate _____ next to somebody who is eating an apple noisily. (sit)

10. Fiona had hoped _____ to university in the summer, but now her dream had disappeared. (go)

11. Can you imagine _____ a car on Sunday and just driving to the coast? (hire)

12. Holly had been learning _____ Braille since the beginning of term. (read)

13. Did you manage _____ the cake decorations that I asked for? (buy)

14. If I were you, I wouldn't mind _____ Marina a few books. (lend)

15. By the end of the holiday we couldn't afford _____ again. (eat out)

16. Will you have practised _____ this piece on the trumpet by the time we meet again next week? (play)

17. Alicia likes _____ in bed for a while before she goes to sleep. (read)

18. I much preferred _____ Manchester compared to Huddersfield. (visit)

19. Charlie has been pretending _____ an urchin from the film *Oliver* all morning. (be)

20. If you would like _____, I would be happy to accompany you. (dance)

GERUND OR INFINITIVE 2

Fill in either a gerund or an infinitive.

1. Please consider _____ your dad to let me borrow his lawnmower. (ask)

2. When the snow began _____, Elena sighed and pressed her nose against the window. (fall)

3. We have decided _____ our bungalow and move to the French Alps. (sell)

4. I think their new production of *Hamlet* really deserves _____ well. (do)

5. Do you fancy _____ that new restaurant that's opened down by the lake? (try)

6. We need _____ ten more tokens before we can get the free watch. (collect)

7. Oliver's grandma had offered _____ care of the dog while they were away. (take)

8. "Have you been watching *The Voice*?" "No, I keep _____ it." (miss)

9. Is George planning _____ his cousin Albert to the family barbecue? (invite)

10. If people had continued _____ CDs, the music industry would be in a better state than it is now. (buy)

11. My brother tends _____ fishing at the weekend. (go)

12. Will you have finished _____ your students' coursework before lunch? (mark)

13. Laurence didn't expect _____ a single card on Valentine's Day. (receive)

14. Michael desperately wanted _____ his car for a more reliable model. (change)

15. Sally missed _____ time with her dad, who was working abroad. (spend)

GERUND OR INFINITIVE 1

1. After two weeks of discussion we have agreed **to give** you the job. (give)
2. You would do well to avoid **taking** the motorway this morning. (take)
3. There would be an outcry if we publicly discussed **privatising** the National Health Service. (privatise)
4. It was tough, but Polly finally admitted **stealing** the jewellery. (steal)
5. If Harold had disliked **eating** the apple pie, I wouldn't have offered him any more. (eat)
6. My daughter sometimes asks me **to help** her with her homework. (help)
7. I think you will really enjoy **meeting** my parents on Friday. (meet)
8. It can't have been easy for Barry to give up **smoking**. (smoke)
9. I hate **to sit / sitting** next to somebody who is eating an apple noisily. (sit)
10. Fiona had hoped **to go** to university in the summer, but now her dream had disappeared. (go)
11. Can you imagine **hiring** a car on Sunday and just driving to the coast? (hire)
12. Holly had been learning **to read** Braille since the beginning of term. (read)
13. Did you manage **to buy** the cake decorations that I asked for? (buy)
14. If I were you, I wouldn't mind **lending** Marina a few books. (lend)
15. By the end of the holiday we couldn't afford **to eat out** again. (eat out)
16. Will you have practised **playing** this piece on the trumpet by the time we meet again next week? (play)
17. Alicia likes **to read / reading** in bed for a while before she goes to sleep. (read)
18. I much preferred **to visit / visiting** Manchester compared to Huddersfield. (visit)
19. Charlie has been pretending **to be** an urchin from the film *Oliver* all morning. (be)
20. If you would like **to dance**, I would be happy to accompany you. (dance)

GERUND OR INFINITIVE 2

1. Please consider **asking** your dad to let me borrow his lawnmower. (ask)
2. When the snow began **to fall / falling**, Elena sighed and pressed her nose against the window. (fall)
3. We have decided **to sell** our bungalow and move to the French Alps. (sell)
4. I think their new production of *Hamlet* really deserves **to do** well. (do)
5. Do you fancy **trying** that new restaurant that's opened down by the lake? (try)
6. We need **to collect** ten more tokens before we can get the free watch. (collect)
7. Oliver's grandma had offered **to take** care of the dog while they were away. (take)
8. "Have you been watching *The Voice*?" "No, I keep **missing** it." (miss)
9. Is George planning **to invite** his cousin Albert to the family barbecue? (invite)
10. If people had continued **to buy / buying** CDs, the music industry would be in a better state than it is now. (buy)
11. My brother tends **to go** fishing at the weekend. (go)
12. Will you have finished **marking** your students' coursework before lunch? (mark)
13. Laurence didn't expect **to receive** a single card on Valentine's Day. (receive)
14. Michael desperately wanted **to change** his car for a more reliable model. (change)
15. Sally missed **spending** time with her dad, who was working abroad. (spend)